WE ARE
WITNESSES

We Are Witnesses

Five Diaries of Teenagers Who Died in the Holocaust

by Jacob Boas

Foreword by Patricia C. McKissack

HENRY HOLT AND COMPANY/ NEW YORK

For Erica, Naomi, Simon, and Patricia

I wish to thank the following for their assistance: Menno Metselaar of the Anne Frank Foundation in Amsterdam; the Netherlands War Documentation Institute, particularly librarians Dick van Galen Last and René Kruis; Ronald Rupp and Peter Davies, for kindnesses innumerable; Joanna Wiszniewicz at the Institute for Jewish History in Warsaw; Hugo de Schampheleire of the Auschwitz Foundation (Brussels); Ewa Rudowska, for showing me around Kielce and Krajno; the YIVO in New York. And for permission to quote from the diaries and the use of photographs, the author is indebted to: Yad Vashem, The Holocaust Martyrs' and Heroes' Remembrance Authority (Jerusalem), publishers of the diaries of Moshe Flinker and Éva Heyman; Beit Lohammei haGghetaot (Ghetto Fighters' House, Israel), publishers of *The Diary of the Vilna Ghetto*; Anne Frank Foundation (Amsterdam) and Anne Frank-Fonds (Basel); Ksiazka i Wieda (Warsaw), publishers of *The Diary of Dawid Rubinowiz*; Doubleday, for *The Diary of Anne Frank: The Critical Edition*. But of all those who have in any way helped me with this book, I am most grateful to my wife. The overall responsibility for the text, needless to say, is mine.

Henry Holt and Company, Inc., *Publishers since 1866*
115 West 18th Street, New York, New York 10011

Henry Holt is a registered
trademark of Henry Holt and Company, Inc.

Library of Congress Cataloging-in-Publication Data
We are witnesses: five diaries of teenagers who died in the Holocaust /
by Jacob Boas.
p.   cm.
Includes bibliographical references.
1. Holocaust, Jewish (1939–1945)—Personal narratives—Juvenile literature. 2. Jewish teenagers—Europe, Eastern—Biography—Juvenile literature. 3. World War, 1939–1945—Children—Europe, Eastern—Juvenile literature. [1. Holocaust, Jewish (1939–1945)—Personal narratives. 2. World War, 1939–1945—Jews. 3. Jews—Biography.] I. Boas, Jacob.
D804.3.W385   1995   940.53'18'0922—dc20   [B]   94-43889

ISBN 0-8050-3702-0
First Edition—1995

Printed in the United States of America
on acid-free paper. ∞
10 9 8 7 6 5 4 3 2 1

Contents

Foreword

I remember reading *The Diary of Anne Frank* one cold winter day when school had been cancelled because of snow. I finished the last few pages just as late afternoon shadows engulfed the room. Hurriedly, I switched on a light, called my children to me, and hugged them tightly. That was twenty-five years ago. Recently, I read *We Are Witnesses*, a collection of five diaries by Jewish teenagers (including Anne Frank), who chronicled their day-to-day ordeals in Nazi-occupied Lithuania, Hungary, Belgium, and Holland between 1940 and 1944. Once again, I was overcome with the need to embrace my loved ones, but more important, I was also moved to tell someone about what I'd read.

Come, meet David, Moshe, Yitzhak, Éva, and Anne, whose diaries are personal accounts of the true horror of the Holocaust. Their stories are intense and, at first, may startle you, even make you feel uncomfortable. Perhaps you'll experience some anger and frustration. That's okay. I sure did. But slowly I came to realize that these young writers weren't messengers of anger and hatred, suffering and dying. Actually, they were ordinary teenagers—much like you, your brother, sister, or friends—seeking a reason why such extraordinarily terrible things were happening to them, their families and friends. Without exception, though, each one clung to hope, and by their examples of courage and strength, bore witness to the resilience of the human spirit.

The Nazis were stopped before they could complete their genocidal plans, but the evil that gave direction to their purpose is still at large in the world. We only need to pick up the newspapers or listen to a news broadcast to hear terms such as "ethnic cleansing," "race superiority," and "ethnic purity." This book, though written by Jews, is not only for Jewish readers. These diaries stand as a direct challenge to *all* race hatred, then and now. They passionately illustrate what happens when human rights are violated and nobody speaks up. They detail the process by which extremism corrupts justice and mocks mercy. We might all heed the statement by Martin Niemoller (1892–1964), a German pastor, who summarizes the important lesson we can all learn from the tragedy of the Holocaust:

In Germany, the Nazis came for the Communists and I didn't speak up because I was not a Communist. Then they came for the Jews and I didn't speak up because I was not a Jew. Then they came for the labor unionists and I didn't speak up because I was not a labor unionist. Then they came for the Catholics and I was a Protestant so I didn't speak up. Then they came for me. . . . By that time there was no one to speak up for anyone.

After you have been guided through these personal accounts by Jacob Boas, who is a survivor of a Nazi concentration camp, my hope is that you will take time to reflect, to look inward, then perhaps reach out. It is my belief that when you've read the last page, that's when the stories really begin.

Patricia C. McKissack
St. Louis, Missouri
January 1, 1995

We Are
Witnesses

Introduction

". . . and I believe that the child is possessed by a flame more powerful than any force that endeavors to destroy our people."

Adolf Hitler set out to change the world from the ground up. The German leader dreamed of creating an empire that would last a thousand years and declared that millions of Jewish men, women, and children would have to be killed to bring it about. When the gas stopped pouring and the guns fell silent, six million Jews lay dead. A fourth of these were children.

But for luck, I would have shared their fate. My birth certificate states that I was born on November 1, 1943, in Westerbork, a small farming community in the northeast of Holland. But the certificate is misleading. My first home was a barracks—Barrack 50, to be exact—in the Nazi camp named for the town. From Westerbork, ninety-three trains carried the bulk of Holland's Jews to their deaths in extermination camps located in Poland. The ninety-third, and last, train carried Anne Frank.

The Nazis justified the murder of children on the ground that it was impossible to destroy a weed without yanking out the root. Since children were the "germ cell" from which a new Jewish danger could grow, their destruction was considered a must. Without it, the Nazis asserted, the war could not be won, the Jew would conquer the world, and "his crown," Hitler wrote in *Mein Kampf* ("My Struggle"), the bible of the Nazi movement, would "become the funeral wreath of humanity."

Hitler blamed the Jews for creating the moral code based on the commandment to love one's neighbor, and for giving birth to Christianity. He considered the ethical teachings of Judaism and Christianity to run counter to humankind's true nature and to be obstacles to Nazi world domination. In their stead, Hitler and his followers glorified power and bloodshed and preached the doctrine of "Aryan" (by which he meant northern European gentile) superiority—the myth of the "master race."

When the Nazis came to power in 1933, Jews had been living in Germany for more than a thousand years. The first Jews had come to Europe in the aftermath of the first-century Roman conquest of Palestine, the ancient homeland of the Jews. The Romans adopted Christianity as the official religion of their empire in the fourth century. In the centuries that followed the collapse of the Roman Empire, Jews did not have an easy time of it. Christians blamed them for the crucifixion of Jesus and passed laws that kept them from owning land or weapons, or entering certain occupations. The Lateran Council of 1215 decreed that Jews had to mark their clothes with a badge, and fifty years later they were compelled to live in ghettos, city quarters isolated from Christian society.

Although Jews endured numerous waves of persecution in Christian Europe, including expulsion from some countries (England in the twelfth century and Spain in the fifteenth) and wholesale slaughter in others (France and Germany in the eleventh century), there had never been a policy to kill each and every one of them, as in Hitler's Germany. As the centuries passed and the hold of religion waned, many Jews believed that the worst was behind them.

In the nineteenth century, Western European Jews received the same rights as other citizens and quickly entered the mainstream—too quickly, some of their enemies said. More and more Jews shed their religion, or kept their ties to a minimum, and married outside the faith. Others found a new "faith" in socialism, which saw a bond among all working people that cut across national boundaries.

The very success of Jews in establishing their presence in Western Europe, be it in business, or as university professors, publishers, writers, or doctors, also produced a backlash. Now they were no longer attacked for religious beliefs, or for their supposed complicity in the crucifixion of Jesus, but were condemned as a race. Jews were branded as an alien, dangerous, and "indigestible" people. Hitler brought this development to its fateful conclusion.

Under the old-style Christian anti-Semitism, a Jew

who converted was no longer a Jew but a full-fledged member of the Christian community. This was no longer possible under racial theories that held that a person's intellectual, moral, and physical traits were fixed for all time: A leopard cannot change its spots. Hitler believed that the world had entered a crucial phase—it would be Aryan or it would be Jewish—and that God had sent him to secure the victory for the master race: "By warding off the Jews I am fighting for the Lord's work," he wrote.

The most important players in this power struggle were children. "Give me the youth and I have the future," Hitler declared. The German leader planned on founding special schools known as *Ordensburgen* to realize his vision of the ideal Aryan male (girls were considered inferior to boys and their future was as housekeepers and breeders). "In my *Ordensburgen*," Hitler boasted, "a youth will grow up before which the world will shrink back. A violently active, dominating, intrepid, brutal youth—that is what I am after. Youth must be all those things. It must be indifferent to pain. There must be no weakness and tenderness in it. I want to see once more in its eyes the gleam of pride and independence of the beast of prey."

While the Nazi "school for barbarians" taught children to scorn books and to love hatred, to identify might with right, and to believe that the "law of nature" mandated killing the "weak," David, Yitzhak, Moshe, Éva, and Anne kept finding ways to improve their minds and expressed horror at the blood being spilled on all sides, even as they stood in the executioner's shadow. It would never have occurred to them to think of people as "poisonous mushrooms" responsible for all "misery, disease, and death" in the world, as German children were taught to believe about Jews.

The diaries of the Jewish teenagers spell out the anguish of an entire generation. Reading them, however, I was struck by the youngsters' ambition to make something of themselves, their resilience and high-mindedness—and pained by their sadness and humiliation, their loneliness and helplessness, and the grief they felt when friends were cut down. Yet they kept on dreaming, moving forward, preparing to make their way in the world as photographers, diplomats, writers, historians, and workers. Their lives, brief as they were, testify to the existence of that holy spark Moshe Flinker believed burned in each person's soul.

Éva, David, Moshe, Yitzhak, and Anne were able to rise above hatred and hold on to their humanity. "It's twice as hard for us young ones to hold our ground, and maintain our opinions, in a time when all ideals are being shattered and destroyed, when people are showing their worst side, and do not know whether to believe in truth and right and God," wrote Anne in her diary two weeks before she and her family were betrayed. The ability of the young people presented in this book to cling to "truth and right and God," despite everything they had to endure, must be accounted the highest form of resistance.

The Jews of Poland were the first to experience the full brunt of the Nazi terror. On September 21, 1939, a week before Poland's surrender, Reinhard Heydrich, chief of the German Security Police and Security Service, dispatched an express letter to his Special Action Squads in Poland informing them of the measures to be taken against the Jews there. For now, Jews were to be collected "in as few concentration points as possible . . . in cities which are rail junctions, or at least are located along railroad lines." The police chief "with the heart of iron" further decreed that in every community with a substantial number of Jews, a council of Jewish elders composed of influential persons and rabbis be set up to help "evacuate" the Jews from the countryside. The councils were to be made "fully responsible for . . . the exact and punctual execution of all directives issued or yet to be issued." The "concentration points" were in fact ghettos, many of them completely sealed off from the world.

Regulations designed to hedge Jews in were not long in coming. The first one stipulated that "Jews resident in the Government General [the newly created administrative area covering central and southern Poland] are obliged to work." Jewish physicians could no longer treat Aryan patients, and vice versa. Jews could not slaughter animals in accordance with Jewish dietary laws. They had to stay home between 9 P.M. and 5 A.M. and wear the "star of Zion" at all times. They could not draw their pensions, or dispose of their savings as they saw fit, or buy gold or other precious metals; they had to declare and register everything they owned. They were not allowed to change residence without first obtaining permission from the German authorities, travel on trains, or use other modes of transportation.

It is at this point, approximately, that David Rubin-owicz started keeping a journal. David, the son of a dairyman, was from Krajno, a small village in the Polish countryside. He was twelve years old.

Seven months later it was May 1940 and Holland's turn to fall to the Nazis. Holland's long-standing reputation for tolerance led the Germans to proceed gradually. "Our freedom was strictly limited," wrote Anne Frank of this period. "Yet things were still bearable." But after two years the dam burst, and a flood of measures similar to those instituted in Poland washed over the Dutch Jewish community. Sensing that the curtain was about to come down, the Franks, in Amsterdam, and the Flinkers, who were living in The Hague, decided to go into hiding. The Franks prepared to move into the house on the Prinsen-gracht; the Flinkers went to Brussels, Belgium. In Brussels, Moshe Flinker, one of eight children, lived in semihiding. He changed his name, went to school, and started studying Arabic on his own, preparing to become a diplomat in the future state of Israel. He was fifteen.

With the invasion of the Soviet Union in June of 1941, the fate of the Jews was sealed and by mid-1942 the "Final Solution to the Jewish Question" was well under way. One of the areas Germany annexed after smashing into the U.S.S.R. in 1941 was the Soviet republic of Lithuania and its capital, Vilna (now Vilnius). Vilna was home to Yitzhak Rudashevski. No need to go slow here. Within a matter of months, thousands of Jews were taken out and shot at Ponar, a leafy area just outside the city. When Nazi tanks rolled into Vilna,

Yitzhak was thirteen years old, a student at a Jewish secondary school, and an ardent communist.

On March 31, 1944, Anne Frank wrote: "Hungary is occupied by German troops. There are still a million Jews there, so they too will have had it now." Éva Heyman was one of those. The month before, she had turned thirteen and received her first pair of high heels. Éva dreamed of becoming a photographer and marrying an Englishman. With Germany headed for defeat, Adolf Eichmann, the man in charge of routing Jews to their final destination, organized the ghettoization of the Hungarian provinces on an "assembly-line" basis before "purging" them in "the most ruthless deportation and massacre program of the war." Éva Heyman arrived in Auschwitz in June.

Anne arrived in Auschwitz a month before Éva's death. At the end of October, Anne was taken to Bergen-Belsen, Germany, where she died of hunger and disease, in March 1945, just weeks before liberation.

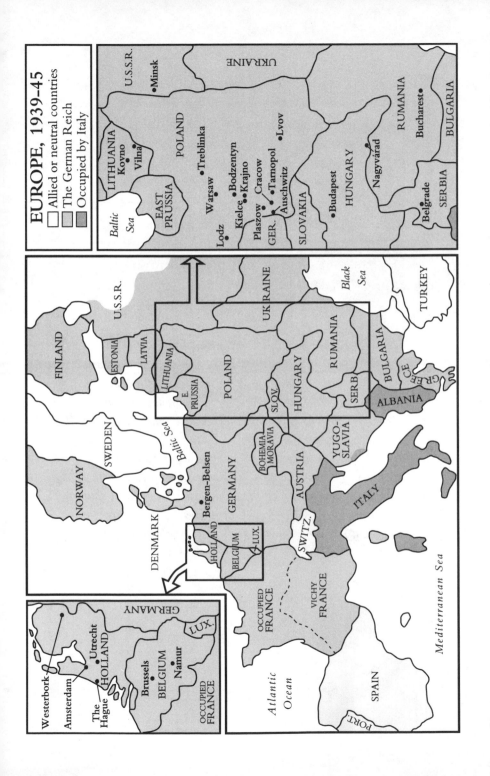

EUROPE, 1939–45

☐ Allied or neutral countries
▨ The German Reich
■ Occupied by Italy

The militia was in Slupia and arrested three Jews. They finished them off in Bieliny (they were certainly shot). Already a lot of Jewish blood has flowed in this Bieliny, in fact a whole Jewish cemetery has already grown up there. When will this bloodshed finally end? If it goes on much longer, then people will drop like flies out of sheer horror. A peasant from Krajno came to tell us our former neighbor's daughter had been shot because she'd gone out after seven o'clock. I can scarcely believe it, but everything's possible. A girl as pretty as a picture—if she could be shot, then the end of the world will soon be here.

Photo taken from the film Dawids Tagebuch. Courtesy of Bundesarchiv Berlin

CHAPTER 1

David Rubinowicz

"The End of the World Will Soon Be Here"

The Nazis considered Poles subhuman and, after crushing the country "like a soft-boiled egg" in the fall of 1939, treated them with contempt. Young Poles, if allowed to live at all, were to be raised as beasts of burden, with just enough education as "would demonstrate to them the hopelessness of their national destiny." Beneath them were the Jews. "They must go"; they had to be "finish[ed] off," proclaimed Governor-General Hans Frank, the new power in Poland.

The killers were not to pass over any place, however small, or any person, however young. And so they swept into Krajno, a small village a hundred miles south of Warsaw, and laid their hands on David Rubinowicz. Today there are few reminders of David, who was fifteen when he disappeared into the gas chambers. No school bears his name; no tablet or plaque of any description marks his brief time on Earth. No grave. The house he lived in no longer stands. All that remains is the diary he kept for two years. That, and a photograph. The photograph was taken during a school outing—the year was 1937, and David was in the fourth grade.

Germany attacked Poland on September 1, 1939. Right away came a decree forbidding Jewish children to attend school. "When I think of how I used to go to school," David wrote in his diary on August 2, 1940, "I feel like bursting into tears, and today I must stay at home and can't go anywhere." He had just turned thirteen.

David was born on July 27, 1927, in Kielce. He had a younger brother, Herszel, and a little sister named Malka. His parents were Josek and Tauba. The five of them shared a small wooden house on Krajno's main road. The Rubinowiczes were country folk, no different from their neighbors, except that they happened to be Jews. Josek Rubinowicz was a dairyman; he owned a cow and a wagon, and ran a small shop. But a year after the German occupation, the dairy was no more. The cow had been sold so the Germans wouldn't take it, and now the Rubinowiczes were much poorer.

"WE'RE UTTERLY UNEMPLOYED"

David had an uncle in Kielce whom he used to visit regularly, and the Rubinowiczes had lived there themselves before moving to Krajno. Like many Polish cities and towns, Kielce had a large Jewish population—in 1939, every fourth person was a Jew. On April 4,

1940, David went to see his uncle again. He got up earlier than usual and left after breakfast. On his right arm he wore "the four-inch armband in white with the star of Zion" all Jews over the age of ten had been ordered to display, at all times, on pain of imprisonment. As Jews were not allowed to travel on vehicles, he walked.

> It was sad following the paths across the fields all by myself. After four hours I was in Kielce. When I went into Uncle's house, I saw them all sitting so sad, and I learned that Jews from various streets are being deported and I also grew sad.

The following day he wrote in his diary: "I couldn't sleep all night, such strange thoughts kept coming into my head."

At first, the effect of the war on the Rubinowiczes was mainly economic. "Today's the first anniversary of the outbreak of war," recorded David on September 1, 1940.

> I remember what we've already gone through in this short time, how much suffering we've already experienced. Before the war everyone had some kind of occupation, hardly anyone was out of work. But in present-day wars ninety percent are unemployed, and only ten percent have a job. Take us—we used to have a dairy and now we're utterly unemployed. There's only very little stock left from before the war, we're still using it up, but it's already running out, and then we don't know what we'll do.

That first year, and even for much of the second, there was still time to have fun. He began learning to ride a bicycle, but had to give it up when its owner would no longer teach him. He could even go out into the woods. "Some boys who were going picking berries in the woods, called for us," he wrote on July 11, 1941. "We took a bowl along. Once there, we immediately began picking bilberries, only the midges and flies stung us badly. We filled the bowl and went home. We got five liters [a little more than a gallon] to start with."

David loved the outdoors, and when he could not go out, there was always the window, where he liked to sit. The window faced the road beyond the yard, and beyond the road lay the fields. "It was nice looking out like that, when I hadn't looked out of the window for a whole week," he reported on July 7, 1940, after a bout of the flu. Four days later: "I feel well already. I went out into the yard; the sun was shining and it was hot. I stayed out the whole day, because I couldn't stand being indoors." Soon, fully recovered, he rejoiced: "Each day I get happier after this illness. Just as the days now get happier and sunnier."

On March 24, 1941, David stood at the window and watched soldiers pass. "My head was awhirl with so many vehicles and cavalry. Heavy artillery was also on the move. It was fun. . . . We hardly ever see soldiers in our parts."

The fun did not last long. A few months later David was home by himself when German militiamen entered the house, searched "every corner," and announced that his father was to report to the militia. Both parents went.

I looked out the window for hours on end, thinking they'll soon be back, but the hours went by and still no sign of them. All sorts of ideas went through my mind—whether they'd been arrested, whether such militia didn't really exist. In the end I didn't know what to think.

Someone told him that his father had been taken into "temporary custody," and David "raced home with this bad news." At the time, his uncle, aunt, and grandmother were living with them. "All were alarmed. Uncle went to the militia right away, and Auntie as well. We children stayed behind on our own, except for Grandma. We had no supper at all; at twelve o'clock I went to bed."

Josek and Tauba had been taken to jail and were released the next day.

On June 17, 1941, the day after Josek and Tauba were taken into "temporary custody," the Rubinowiczes scurried to hide their valuables, linen, and clothing.

There was a terrible panic in the village, as if bandits were coming. And then they came. First they searched a peasant's house, and then they left. When they were near to our house, I thought my heart would jump out, it was thumping so violently, but thank goodness, the militia didn't enter the house, though they certainly meant to. But I said, If they come back, they're bound to search our house. We were so afraid, we didn't know what was happening.

"I WAS SO FRIGHTENED"

The Germans were a constant threat. One showed up at the family's door with a motorcycle that had broken down near the house. "He couldn't leave it just anywhere, so he pushed it into our hall," explained David. "Just then along came some Jews who were on their way to Bodzentyn, and this militiaman began checking their papers, and in the process a Jew received a severe beating from him." Another militiaman, starting to feel cold, just popped into their house to warm himself. "When he was inside, he said the Jews in Krajno should buy two sheepskins for him to make up into a fur coat." On leaving, the German gave his mother a small bottle of vodka.

The militia came often.

December 26, 1941

Father was just dressing when a boy came up to him and told him to go into the shop, a militiaman was calling for him, but it isn't clear why. Father finished dressing and went into the shop. We were very frightened because we didn't know why he'd called for him. Nowadays a person can be arrested for any trifle.

January 15, 1942

While I was having my dinner, I saw the same militiaman who'd been at our place, walking along the street. I ran out into the fields, fleeing because I thought he was coming to fetch us. Out in the fields I thought I'd go to another village and stay there until they left. I set off; then I saw that the militiaman was walking in the same direction as myself. I couldn't run away, because he'd already seen me. I resigned myself to my fate, took off the armband so that at least he wouldn't recognize me from a distance, and carried on walking. When I entered the village, I thought I'd have a stroke, I was so frightened. I then went down the village street. At the other end of the village I met the same militiaman again, because he hadn't been going after me but had come up the other street. He didn't see me, however. You can imagine how terrified I was. He went past and I went home.

February 9, 1942

We had to shovel snow till evening. Father came from Kielce just as the German and the committee entered our house. They didn't make an exact search of the house. As they were leaving, they demanded two chickens and a bottle of vodka for supper. We had to hand them over a chicken and a bottle of vodka. So one day follows another—always expense and fear.

To the Rubinowiczes every German was a whip poised to strike, for a German could do anything—rob, beat, kill—and no questions would be asked. On November 1, 1941, notices went up in Kielce announcing the death penalty for any Jew who entered or left the ghetto without permission. The edict soon covered all the ghettos of the Government General, as the area that used to be Poland had been renamed. Shortly thereafter, David saw a sudden increase in murders, and his fear grew.

December 12, 1941

Yesterday afternoon I went to Bodzentyn to get my tooth filled and intended to stay there overnight. Early this morning the militia came. As they were driving along the highway, they met a Jew who was going out of town, and they immediately shot him for no reason, then they drove on and shot a Jewess, again for no reason. So two victims have perished for absolutely no reason. All the way home I was very frightened I might run across them, but I didn't run across anybody.

December 28, 1941

I was awakened from sleep by a knock on the window; I dressed and went to open the door. It was two Jews from Bodzentyn who were going to Kielce and had come to warm themselves. I asked them for news, and they said two more victims had been shot at Christmas, for no reason either. . . . In the afternoon the clerk of the Jewish elders' council came from Daleszyce and said there'd been five victims that day, five Jews killed by the militia because someone had reported them for hiding furs. The militiaman ordered them to be buried in a hole in their own yard. They were a father, three sons, and a daughter. In Kielce several people fall victim every day for leaving the Jewish Quarter. Under such terrible, bad conditions, days and weeks pass full of fear and terror.

January 8, 1942

In the afternoon I learned that there'd been two more Jewish victims in Bodzentyn. One was killed outright and the other wounded. They arrested the wounded man and took him to the local police in Bieliny, and there they'll probably beat him to death.

January 15, 1942

I learned that they'd manacled a Jew and taken him to the local police. . . . They'd tied him to their sleigh and he'd been forced to run after it. Perhaps they'll shoot him—who knows? We sat there the whole evening, very sad and thoughtful. How many enemies are on the prowl after such a poor defenseless creature! . . . While he was tied to the sleigh, he couldn't run anymore, and they'd dragged him along behind the sleigh and then shot him—such an unhappy fate he'd had to suffer!

In March 1942, the Rubinowiczes were forced to move to the nearby town of Bodzentyn.

March 16, 1942

Someone at home said that in Krajno four Jewish persons had been shot while walking in the direction of Kielce. Two persons had only been wounded with bayonets, and two, a mother and son, were dead. When you hear endlessly of such atrocities, how can you live calmly, without fear? When you hear such things you really do get very frightened.

April 10, 1942

The militia was in Slupia and arrested three Jews. They finished them off in Bieliny (they were certainly shot). Already a lot of Jewish blood has flowed in Bieliny; in fact a whole Jewish cemetery has already grown up there. When will this bloodshed finally end? If it goes on much longer, then people will drop like flies out of sheer horror. A peasant from Krajno came to tell us our former neighbor's daughter had been shot because she'd gone out after seven o'clock. I can scarcely believe it, but everything's possible. A girl as pretty as a picture—if she could be shot, then the end of the world will soon be here.

June 1, 1942

This morning two Jewish women, a mother and a daughter, had gone into the country. Unfortunately the Germans were driving from Rudki to Bodzentyn to fetch potatoes and ran across them. When the two women caught sight of the Germans they began to flee, but they were overtaken and arrested. They intended shooting them on the spot in the village, but the mayor wouldn't allow it. They then went into the woods and shot them there.

One of Hitler's major goals was to make hatred of Jews permanent. On February 12, 1942, David noticed the village policeman putting up a notice.

On it a Jew is shown, mincing meat and putting a rat into the mincer. Another is pouring water from a

bucket into the milk. In the third picture, a Jew is shown stamping dough with his feet, and worms are crawling over him and the dough. The heading of the notice read: "The Jew Is a Cheat, Your Only Enemy!" And the inscription ran as follows:

> Dear reader, before your very eyes,
> Are Jews deceiving you with lies.
> If you buy your milk from them, beware,
> Dirty water they've poured in there.
> Into the mincer dead rats they throw,
> Then as mincemeat it's put on show.
> Worms infest their homemade bread,
> Because the dough with feet they tread.

David stuck around long enough to register the reaction of the people standing around. They laughed, and their laughter, he wrote, "gave me a headache from the shame that the Jews suffer nowadays. God grant that this shame may soon end."

EVACUATION

The biggest change in David's life was announced in January of 1942. Sitting at his window "watching the wind blowing across the fields," he spotted the village crier and "went to see what was the news." What he heard sent him dashing home: "All Jews were to be evacuated from all the villages."

"Evacuation" of Jews had been going on practically

since the German invasion almost two and a half years earlier, but till then the Rubinowiczes had been spared. "Now it's our turn to suffer," realized David. "How long, God only knows." Five days after learning that the seven Jewish families of Krajno were to be "evacuated," Krajno's mayor showed up at the house. "Father fetched some vodka and they finished it off together because he was a bit chilled." The mayor "said all Jews would have to be shot because they were enemies," and other things that took David's breath away. "If I could only write down a part of all he said at our house, but I simply can't."

Josek spent the final months in Krajno in a frantic, but doomed, effort to convince the regional Jewish council to postpone their "resettlement." The Jewish council administered the affairs of the Jewish community; it was created by the Nazis and answered to them. "We've put ourselves in God's hands and are ready for anything," wrote David at the end of this period.

The Rubinowiczes sold off items that were no longer needed; they retrieved the iron stove they had lent out; they hauled wood and ran errands; they laid in half a hundredweight of potatoes ("It's always cheaper to buy things in a village than in a town"), and David "took down the extension to the cowshed—it'll provide wood for a few days."

When the day of the "relocation" arrived, it became clear just how well Josek and his wife, Tauba, were thought of in the village. The neighbors remembered their readiness to offer assistance to anyone, Jew and non-Jew alike. "There's hardly anyone in our village

who's not sorry for us," David recorded in his diary on March 10, 1942. "Many don't even want to come and see us—they say they don't want to witness other people's misfortune." But others came anyway and wished them well. "Thinking of how we had to leave here, I had to go out into the yard. I cried so much that I stood there sobbing more than half an hour. When I'd quieted down a bit, I went back into the house. The peasants had already gone."

David's neighbors did not behave like the Jew-hating Poles of legend. His diary is filled with instances of Poles going out of their way to help Jews. Poles repeatedly tipped off Jews when Germans were out for blood, and just as often David ducked into peasant homes to stay out of the Germans' clutches. This was true in Bodzentyn as well as in Krajno. In the tension-filled days of the following May, for example, when the German militia, the Polish police, and even the Jewish police were rounding up Jews for labor camps, David constantly relied on the help of non-Jews to avoid being captured.

The next morning a man came with a cart and the Rubinowiczes loaded their things. "When the carter had gone, it was as empty at home as a tunnel." David said good-bye to the uncle and aunt who had been staying with them—they were going to Bieliny—and he helped them load their stuff as well. "This evening was very sad; there was no one here, only myself, Mother, and Father."

After the house had been turned into an empty shell, David wished he was already gone. March 12 was the day. Early in the morning, David and his father went to get a cart. An hour later a peasant showed up with a horse. David walked the six and a half miles between Krajno and Bodzentyn in a daze, choking on emotions.

> I went out without any armband on. As I left, I couldn't say a word, my heart was so heavy. I walked perhaps five kilometers [three miles], almost unconscious—I didn't know how I managed to walk so fast. The whole way the cart couldn't catch up with me. En route I was terribly frightened—oh, God, if anybody had met us then!

FORCED LABOR

Bodzentyn was much bigger than Krajno, with houses viciously crammed together. The area the Germans had designated as the Jewish ghetto was particularly depressing. There the houses were older, uglier, and smaller, and the cobblestones higher. No wonder David felt stifled in Bodzentyn. Though his Jewish neighbors treated his family "like brothers," he had a hard time getting used to his new surroundings: Bodzentyn was not home. Here there were no fields to run through, no forest to roam, no mushrooms to gather. "Here I go out into the street, but in no time at all I'm back—what's there for me to do in the street?"

David missed Krajno terribly, and he would see it just one more time. He went there on April 28 with his father, scrounging for food.

While we were going along, I felt exactly as if I was going home, and soon I found myself lost in day-dreams. But shortly after, I realized they were only idle reveries. Arriving, Father went to the village and I waited at our former neighbor's. Later I went to our house; there Father was waiting for me. When I went in, the dwelling seemed so strange, as if we'd never lived there. Father gave me money to pay for the po-tatoes he'd bought. How glad I was to run along the path I knew so well! And again I felt as if I was just running back home, that my parents were there and all the others, but then it was all over. When I got back, Father was no longer there. I baked a few potatoes for myself and waited for him. Then I sat down at the window, specially to recall better the moments I'd once spent there. But I didn't sit for long. Somehow I felt so sad that I went out; otherwise I'd have wept.

In Bodzentyn the world of the Rubinowiczes com-pletely unraveled. First they were robbed. "One misfortune—that's easily borne, it is not until several combine that a human being is crushed," reflected Da-vid. Then came the manhunts. The first anti-Jewish decree issued in Poland required "all Jews to work." Jews between the ages of twelve and sixty-nine had to register with the local Jewish community leaders. Shirkers faced up to ten years of imprisonment. This "work" was forced labor, not unlike that performed by chain gangs in some prisons in the American South, only worse.

The raids intensified after the Rubinowiczes were forced to relocate to Bodzentyn. Bodzentyn had a Jew-ish council, and one of its main tasks was to supply the

Germans with Jewish labor. The council, however, had a tough time filling the orders, since Jews naturally tended to stay away. It was then that the militia and the Polish police, and sometimes the Jewish police as well, sprang into action, combing the streets and seizing Jews in their homes.

March 19, 1942

Today there've been rumors circulating that on Sunday six squads of Polish police are coming, plus the militia. Some say they'll be making raids, others say otherwise; no one really knows. Raids of course not on Aryans, only on Jews. Everyone goes around frightened, wondering where he can hide and find somewhere safe. But where can one feel safe nowadays? Nowhere at all.

April 14, 1942

Early in the morning, I learned that the militia had come to search through the Jews' dwellings. They've taken away three people from one house. . . . We were very frightened they'd perhaps visit us . . . and even though we don't own anything, we were very frightened. . . . While I was sitting at home, I saw a militiaman go past, and someone went into Auntie's place. I went to the stairway and heard the Germans were with Auntie and a policeman had come in from the yard. My heart began pounding like a hammer. I didn't go home, but instead walked along the street slowly.

May 6, 1942

About three o'clock I was awakened by knocking. It was the police already making a raid. I wasn't afraid. After all, Father and my cousin were in Krajno and knew what was going on. The other cousins had hidden. After a few minutes, I heard more knocking on the door and Uncle opened up right away. A Jewish and a Polish policeman entered. Immediately they began making a search; one of them eyed me and ordered me to get dressed. The other asked how old I was. I answered fourteen; then he left me alone. They rummaged around a bit, found no one. . . . I wasn't afraid; even so I was trembling as if I had a fit of the shivers.

May 8, 1942

Auntie came, saying they're also picking up people like me. At first I didn't know what to do, but then suddenly realized I had to hide. I went to our Polish neighbor's wife and stayed there. The slightest rustling, and I was terrified it was them coming in!

May 15, 1942

At 4 A.M. several trucks arrived. We thought, Now they'll quickly be evacuating everyone. I got so scared, I got a terrible pain and had to go outside. Scarcely had I opened the door but I saw a German standing on the other side of the street, looking straight at me. I didn't go out but left the door open. I was very frightened, scared he'd come into our flat.

Though he was eligible for work himself, David worried most about his father. Every time Josek left the house, David was terrified. Had he been picked up in a raid? Where had he been taken? Did he have enough to eat, did he have his medicine? Would he return?

Still, David kept his head. What's more, he often was less flustered than others. A few weeks after moving to Bodzentyn, the Rubinowiczes "were robbed of everything": "three geese . . . fifteen kilos [about thirty-three pounds] rye, five kilos [eleven pounds] flour, and eight loaves." Devastated, they questioned a man who had been seen casing the house, but he denied everything. "I suggested we should go to his brother's place—perhaps there'd be some clue there. . . . There *was* a clue—near the house there were bloodstains everywhere. . . . He confessed everything and returned the lot."

David was extremely conscientious. He rarely reported anything he had not personally experienced or was unable to check for himself. When a boy told him that a German had ordered snow to be shoveled into a Jew's house "because it was so dirty inside," David did not believe it. "In the evening, however, I went and saw with my own eyes that it was really true." A stickler for accuracy, he routinely checked and double-checked his sources. Instead of saying "four Jewish persons had been shot while walking in the direction of Kielce," he wrote, "Someone at home said that in Krajno four Jewish persons had been shot. . . ." Even the militia benefited from David's evenhandedness. When they turned Krajno inside out requisitioning food, David followed them and saw them entering a house, but whether they took anything he would not say—"because I don't know."

The brutal acts of the German enforcers in the Polish countryside took up many an entry, but David also recorded those rare moments when the soldiers appeared to him in a human light. The militia had been "quite decent," he commented after one of their frequent raids; "they hadn't bawled at a single person," and paid eighty zlotys for the bicycle they took from his cousin, "and my cousin had to sign for it." They didn't take anything from his cousin's sister, "only the five meters [a little over five yards] of material because they simply had to confiscate the material." On one occasion Jews even sent a cart with "presents for the militia because they were kind people." David also had nice things to say about the German who helped his mother retrieve the things the militia had seized in a raid, as well as for the militiaman who "tore his hair" because he was sorry for what he had done—shooting a person on the run. On April 21, 1942, David reported that his uncle had to pay a fine of twenty zlotys for failure to clear the yard of manure, but added: "I didn't actually hear that myself."

A TERRIBLE DAY

Living under the gun took its toll. Murders "for no reason," arrests "for any trifle," and humiliations and beatings and requisitionings and roundups and fear, always fear. "If only you could have one quiet day," he wrote on April 19, 1942. "My nerves are utterly exhausted; whenever I hear of anyone's distress, I burst into tears, my head starts aching, and I'm exhausted, as if I'd been doing the hardest possible work. It's not only me; everyone feels the same."

Everyone included his family. "Uncle and the others in the house nag us constantly. We're not even allowed to chop wood in the yard, and on top of that various trivial things that really aren't worth mentioning. But we live at a time when you can't speak out; all you can do is keep quiet and swallow everything."

Everyone included his mother, going to pieces before his eyes. "Mother is as exhausted by today's events as if they'd been going on for a whole month," David wrote about the day she spent at the police trying to get back the things that had been taken from them in a raid. One day, after her husband had been taken to a labor camp and the Jewish council kept giving her the runaround, she came home, "her eyes red with weeping," and "the whole day [went] around crying. You can well imagine how I feel."

Everyone included his father. Josek Rubinowicz was an old-fashioned man, accustomed to obedience and by nature somewhat irritable. The strain on the head of the household was enormous. One day Josek Rubinowicz's nerves snapped. May 1, 1942:

While I was in Krajno I got several clumps of chives. Today I had time to plant them in flowerpots. I still wasn't finished when Father called me to help with the grinding. I was to leave everything in the yard just as it was—my brother could clear up. After grinding, I went into the flat. When Father came, he began to be very angry at me—why had I scattered the wood all over the woodshed?—and beat me. I told him I hadn't had time to tidy up the wood, and he beat me even more. I was very upset at him beating me without cause. And finally, when he'd beaten me so hard several times with his belt buckle, I began crying, not so much out of pain as anger. I got real bruises that hurt badly. Finally he ordered me to start grinding. But how could I grind when my arm hurt so much I couldn't move it?

Now it was David's turn to snap. "Father doesn't love me at all, and he wouldn't be sorry if something happened to me. All he feels is his duty; it doesn't cross his mind there might be more to it than that."

David could not forget the beating, nor the thoughts he had about his father. May 6: "A terrible day!" Their place had been ransacked, their food seized, and, worst of all, the eldest Rubinowicz was picked up in a raid. Filled with remorse, David sobbed, "They've taken Father from us, they've taken our property, and now I feel such a yearning for Father. . . ."

Two trucks came up and one had a trailer. When I saw it I immediately thought they were taking Father away in it, and began weeping terribly. How can you help weeping. Father told my brother he should bring him food, some clothes, and a little mug. And again I couldn't help crying when I saw him taking those things. . . . The truck was already at the other market-place. I burst out crying, and as they came up, I cried out: "Papa! Papa, where are you? If only I could see you once more." . . . And then I saw him on the last truck; his eyes were red with weeping. I kept on look-ing at him until he disappeared round the corner; then I had a sudden fit of crying, and I felt how much I love him and how much he loves me. And only now did I feel that what I wrote on May 1 about him not loving me was a beastly lie, and who knows if I won't have to pay for doubting him when it wasn't true at all? . . . I cried a very long time, and every time I thought of Father's tear-stained face, I began sobbing all over again. The dearest person in the whole world we had, they've taken away from us—and ill as well. . . .

Josek Rubinowicz had been taken to Skarzysko Kamienna, a forced-labor camp located twenty miles north of Bodzentyn operated by a German explosives manufacturer. Josek was put to work felling trees and digging up stumps. Contact was maintained with his family via the Jewish council, which shuttled back and forth with parcels, dirty laundry, letters, and money. The first news from him came four days after his cap-ture. It was a letter delivered by a man on a bicycle who identified himself as the overseer of Jews in Skarzysko. "Many people gathered immediately around." The letter said that Josek was well, that the work was tolerable, and that he worried about David. David recorded his father's instructions: "At all costs they shouldn't pick me up. I was to see I hid well." Josek asked for money and food, and that "things be sold off to rescue him." In a subsequent letter, David's father again urged him to hide: "He wants me to put on girl's clothes."

Despite all this, David continued to have mixed feelings about his father. "Why has such a terrible fate befallen my father?" he asked himself six days after Josek was seized. "Perhaps God is giving him his deserts." At the same time, he missed his father terribly. "Not an instant passes but I think of Father," he wrote the day after he was taken away. Whenever trucks returned with prisoners, David was the first to rush out, hoping that his father would be on one of them. On May 8, he went to synagogue with his family—"after all, it *is* Friday"—and was overcome with sorrow because his father was not with them. When he got home, he was "dreadfully sad." Somehow the family managed to set the table for the Sabbath. "But when I see Father's place, and he's not sitting there, then grief and sorrow break my heart." That same feeling of utter desolation overwhelmed him two weeks later, during Shavuot, the feast day that celebrates God's giving of the Ten Commandments to Moses. While praying, he

. . . felt a deep yearning for Father. I saw other children standing with their fathers, and the parts of their prayers that they didn't know were told them by their fathers, and who is there to tell me? . . . Only God alone. God, give me good thoughts and lead me in the right way. Never before have I felt my prayers to be such a burden to me as today. How could they have been so before? If only God would allow Father to return safe and sound.

A HAPPY DAY?

Finally David's prayers were answered. After weeks of anxious waiting, after beating a path to the police station and seeing only other men returning; after calls, letters, and cards, and fruitless attempts to raise money to buy his release—after all this, his father finally came back. It was June 1. "A happy day." David was at a neighbor's making slippers for his sister when he "heard a truck approach, and singing."

> I ran out, and right enough! There they were, driving up. From far away you could see them waving their arms, their caps; I saw my father waving too. I threw everything down, ran to meet them, and arrived at the same time as the truck. I immediately took Father's bundle from him, and he got down from the truck. . . . I entered our flat and couldn't even greet Father, I was so glad. No one can imagine our joy, only someone who's been through the same experience will understand. It was all like in a film, we experienced so much almost in a second. The place was immediately full of people—they all came for the good news. Father had injured his arm—that's why they'd let him out. . . . At first I was very frightened, thinking he'd been very badly wounded. It's hard for me to describe everything Father related. The first week was the worst, until he'd got used to things. The work wasn't so terrible, only the discipline; if a man doesn't march well or sing, he gets beaten. Reveille is at 4 A.M.; at 5 P.M. work ends. For thirteen hours at a stretch the men aren't allowed to take a rest; anyone

who sits down receives a terrible beating. There was no end to his account; we stayed up till 2 A.M.—it's impossible to describe how it was. Father didn't look too bad, he'd had as much to eat as he needed.

The "happy day" is the last entry in David's diary. Dated June 1, 1942, the entry breaks off in midsentence. Whether he continued to write in his diary during the three and a half months the Rubinowiczes managed to hold out before being gassed, we do not know. Between September 15 and 21, the Jews of Bodzentyn and those brought there from neighboring towns—5,000 in all—were made to walk the fifteen miles that lay between Bodzentyn and Suchedniow. On Monday, September 21, Yom Kippur, 4,500 of them were crammed into the cattle cars that would take them to Treblinka, the death camp located thirty-five miles northeast of Warsaw.

A document added to the Polish edition of the diary lists the train schedules for the final weeks of September. Schedule 587 informed railroad employees about the number of "special trains" available to transport the "settlers" from the district of Radom, the district in which the town of Suchedniow was located. The train that carried David left Suchedniow at 4:18 P.M. on the 21st, a Monday, and arrived at Treblinka at 11:24 A.M. the next day. In a little over a year, from July 1942 to September 1943, Treblinka swallowed 850,000 Jews. Fewer than forty survived.

We are like animals surrounded by the hunter. The hunter on all sides: beneath us, above us, from the sides. Broken locks snap, doors creak, axes, saws. I feel the enemy under the boards on which I am standing. The light of an electric bulb seeps through the cracks. They pound, tear, break. Soon the attack is heard from another side. Suddenly, somewhere upstairs, a child bursts into tears. A desperate groan breaks forth from everyone's lips. We are lost. A desperate attempt to shove sugar into the child's mouth is of no avail. They stop up the child's mouth with pillows. The mother of the child is weeping. People shout in wild terror that the child should be strangled. The child is shouting more loudly, the Lithuanians are pounding more strongly against the walls. However, slowly everything calmed down by itself. We understand that they have left. Later we heard a voice from the other side of the hideout: You are liberated. My heart beat with such joy! I have remained alive!

Photo courtesy of Kibbutz Lehamei Hagetaot (Ghetto Fighters' House)

CHAPTER 2

Yitzhak Rudashevski

"Long Live Youth!"

Yitzhak Rudashevski was born on December 10, 1927, in Vilna, the son of a typesetter at a Yiddish daily newspaper and a seamstress mother. Today Vilna is Vilnius, the capital of Lithuania. Between Yitzhak's birth and his death in 1943, the city would change hands a number of times. In 1927 it was part of Poland. In the fall of 1939, Lithuania achieved independence and called itself the Lithuanian Republic. The following year the Soviets took over, and a year later, almost to the day, German tanks rolled into the capital, driving the Soviets out. It was the start of a German occupation that would last until the summer of 1944.

Among Jews the world over, Vilna was honored as a center of learning. Fittingly, Vilna's most famous resident had been a scholar. Elijah Ben Solomon Zalman (1720–1797), better known as the Vilna Gaon (genius), was admired for his intellect, rationality, and learning. The Gaon was buried at the heart of historic Jewish

Vilna, in the *shulhoyf,* a concrete courtyard surrounded by synagogues, houses of learning, and a world-famous Jewish library. Devout Jews from around the world came to visit his grave.

Between 1920 and 1939, when Vilna was part of Poland, Jews faced discrimination on every front, from restrictions on businesses to efforts to force them out altogether. But Jews held on, combating every attempt to make them feel inferior, and went their own way. They took care of education, religion, and the poor. Sports enthusiasts founded Jewish clubs, Jewish workers joined Jewish labor organizations, and Jewish writers wrote for Jewish publishers and the Jewish theater. Newspaper stands carried papers and magazines reflecting every shade of Jewish political opinion and religious affiliation.

A major part of the renewal of Jewish life was the revival of Yiddish, a language akin to German but written with Hebrew characters. The teaching of Yiddish was part of the modernizing efforts of Jews who wanted to shake off the dust of the past without forsaking their Jewishness. Instead of attending religious schools, most young Jews, including girls, started going to schools that taught such modern subjects as physical sciences, singing, nature study, and languages; Yiddish was used in the classroom.

Yitzhak was a true product of this spirit. He attended a school that used the new curriculum and wrote his diary in Yiddish. Yitzhak and his fellow Jews in Vilna drew strength from their progressive culture, which helped them fight back when discrimination and persecution turned into murder.

THE RED FLAG OF FREEDOM

Soon after the arrival of the Soviets in 1940, on a hot and sunny day in July, Vilna's communists organized a pep rally. A shirtsleeved band played. The faithful hoisted banners featuring the latest Party slogans. The Vilna Regional Committee of the Communist Party of Lithuania announced that their country had been accepted "into the great family of nations that are building socialism." It was official: the "hated capitalist order" had been routed, everything was in the hands of the people, the "sun of the Stalinist constitution" was here to stay. Take to heart the teachings of "our comrade Stalin," urged the Committee.

Words against hate, exploitation, and oppression, words for friendship and cooperation—they must have gone straight to Yitzhak's heart. This was a language far different from that calling for economic boycott, violence, and expulsion—the anti-Semitic language of the Poles and Lithuanians among whom he had grown up.

Many of Vilna's Jews welcomed Soviet rule. But it was not poverty or anti-Semitism, nor ideological conviction, that had made them do so—they had also welcomed the founding of the Lithuanian Republic in 1939. Lithuanian Jews hoped that the Soviets would protect them from the Germans, who were slaughtering Jews in Poland. The irony was that the Soviets were equally bigoted. The new rulers did everything they could to destroy Jewish Vilna. They banned organizations and political parties, prohibited the teaching of Hebrew and Jewish history; the new laws left Jews even poorer than before. In addition, Soviet authorities shipped five to six thousand Jews to Siberia.

But none of this appeared in Yitzhak's diary. Yitzhak welcomed the Soviets as glorious liberators and tried to be a model young communist. In the summer of 1940, with the Red Army poised to enter Vilna, he "ran several kilometers to meet the first Soviet tank." He was ecstatic. He wore the red star and the red scarf of the Pioneers, the communist scouting movement, and devoured books like *The Ninth of November,* whose hero gleefully sacrificed himself on behalf of the masses. Yitzhak spent an entire day writing a composition on Bernard Kellermann's heroic communist novel.

We see the whole horror of [World War I] which puts such a dark stamp on human life. The Ninth of November, that is the day when the German people, the exhausted soldiers of the front, raised the red flag of freedom. The wrath of the people spilled over into the famished streets. Ackermann, the hero of the book, the front soldier with three wounds in his broad un-buttoned coat—how beautifully, how idealistically his soldier image appears in the light of the revolution! I copied many splendid excerpts: strong eternal words which proclaim the freedom of nations.

On June 21, as Yitzhak was having a "cheerful conversation" with his friend Gabik, a siren began to howl:

The Hitlerites have attacked our land. They have forced a war upon us. And so we shall retaliate, and strike until we shall smash the aggressor on his own soil. I keep looking at the calm Red Army soldier who is standing on guard in our yard. I feel that I can be sure of him, I see he will not perish. He will perhaps be killed, but the star attached to his hat will remain forever.

The day after the German attack, the Red Army soldier was no longer at his post. He was on the run, as was his whole army. Sadly, red star in lapel, Yitzhak watched his heroes pile into their vehicles. Two days later, Yitzhak saw his first German. "At dawn a motorcycle rides through the street. A gray square-rimmed helmet, spectacles, a greatcoat, and a rifle . . . The helmet flashes coldly and evilly." Later that day, head bowed, he watched the rest of the Germans enter, "a black mirage of tanks, motorcycles, machines." When he got home, he hid his tie and fed the stove with books like *The Ninth of November.* The red star in his lapel was already gone. A neighbor had told him to take it off. That night he lay awake for a long time. "I think how defenseless we are, isolated from each other, exposed entirely to the mercy of the Hitlerites."

Where did Yitzhak get his communist fervor? From his teachers, most likely, and especially teacher Mira Bernshteyn. Like many Jews at the time, Mira saw communism as the answer to persecution. She expected communism to restore Yiddish culture and schools. Above all, she saw it as the last bulwark against Nazism. Mira Bernshteyn had been the principal of Yitzhak's school, and he sought her out the day the

Germans entered Vilna. The school was closed, but she was there. "She was sitting in a depressed mood," he wrote afterward. "We understood each other. She advised us to be sure to hide our neckties." The neckties identified them as communists, whom the Nazis despised.

Mira cared deeply about her students. In a book about his experiences in the Vilna ghetto, poet Abraham Sutzkever recalled the day he sat in on a play being staged by her students. Suddenly the show was interrupted by screaming: Outside, Jews were being dragged from their homes and seized on the streets. A bullet whizzed through a window. Mira ran out. When she returned, she said: "Children! Those who want to destroy us are here. Nobody move, nobody cry. Slip out quietly, without making any noise. Let the youngest go first and then the others, according to age." "All night," Sutzkever recalled, "she stood by the door. If the 'kidnappers' were to come, they would find no one besides herself."

This was not what Yitzhak had imagined it would be like when the Germans first entered Vilna. Then, he believed that there had been "some grievous error which will soon be corrected. I imagine life under the Germans as a short provisional period. I look at the entry of the Germans and I am already thinking of their departure. I imagine them fleeing back beaten up without heads. The Red Army is here again." Yitzhak was sure that his Pioneers, the club of ten boys and girls he had helped organize, would have a part in driving the Germans out. The German bombing of Vilna on June 21, 1941, conflicted with a meeting the ten had scheduled, but Yitzhak decided to hold it anyway. "I think about our future life. I think that we Pioneers will not remain aloof in the struggle. I feel that we shall be useful. . . . I had a foreboding that hard tasks await us. The struggle is beginning, the Soviet Union will arise. . . . I carry with me *The Hero in Chains.* We shall read together about Gavroche, the child of the Parisian proletariat who fell on the barricades beside the adult fighters."

SELECTED "LIKE HORSES"

Between the departure of the Soviets and the entrance of the Germans, "a mortal silence weighed on the city." The calm before the storm. Jews stayed home and in cellars, terrified of the Lithuanians and Poles. The Lithuanians especially had not forgotten that many Jews had welcomed Soviet soldiers with open arms, and were eager to get revenge. "I begin to understand the base betrayal of the Lithuanians," commented Yitzhak in his journal. "They shot the Red Army soldiers in the back. They make common cause with the Hitlerite bandits."

The Germans could afford to remain aloof as the locals took revenge on the Jews for having supported the Soviets. Lithuanian and Polish thugs stripped Jewish homes "down to the toilet seats." Lithuanian "captors" went into Jewish homes and dragged out the men and the women. They "drive them to a station and send

them to work," wrote Yitzhak about the early on-
slaught. "Many of them do not return." Those who
disappeared were either murdered by the marauders or
turned over to the Germans for ten rubles. No one was
safe.

> Our hearts are crushed witnessing the shameful scene
> where women and older people are beaten and kicked
> in the middle of the street by small bandits. . . . I stand
> at the window and feel a sense of rage. Tears come to
> my eyes: All our helplessness, all our loneliness lies in
> the streets. There is no one to take our part. And we
> ourselves are so helpless, so helpless! . . . It rains inces-
> santly. We are so sad, so lonely. We are exposed to
> mockery and humiliation.

Eventually the Germans issued many new laws. Jews
now could not use the sidewalks and had to walk single
file on the right side of the street. This was humiliating
enough, but the decree, issued July 4, 1941, ordering
the wearing of "a yellow star of Zion on the left front
and on the back" made Yitzhak feel like a freak.

> I am looking through the window and see before me
> the first Vilna Jews with badges. It was painful to see
> how people were staring at them. The large piece of
> yellow material on their shoulders seemed to be burn-
> ing me and for a long time I could not put on the
> badge. I felt a hump, as though I had two frogs on me.
> I was ashamed to appear in them on the street, not be-
> cause it would be noticed that I am a Jew, but because
> I was ashamed of what [they were] doing to us. I was

ashamed of our helplessness. We will be hung from head to foot with badges and we cannot help each other in any way. It hurt me that I saw absolutely no way out.

But Yitzhak also realized that it was the Germans who should really feel shame.

Now we pay no attention to the badges. The badge is attached to our coats but has not touched our consciousness. We now possess so much consciousness that we can say that we are not ashamed of our badges! Let those be ashamed who have hung them on us. Let them serve as a searing brand to every conscious German who attempts to think about the future of his people.

In the tailor shop, a German said that he wanted " 'to gorge myself like a Jew.' To them the Jew is the embodiment of a hungry person," commented Yitzhak. "They think that a Jew feels only hunger." One day his mother told him about a German woman who told her daughter not to urinate on the floor because that was what Jews in the ghetto often did, since they had no place to relieve themselves. "We have sunk so low," remarked Yitzhak, "that German women make an example of us to their children as unfortunate and suffering people." Observing someone selecting Jews for work: "The German selects a group of healthy men, selects them like horses, looking at the muscles of each, lines them up and orders them to go. The rest dash after him. The German drives them off with his belt. . . ."

PONAR

On July 4, 1941, a car stopped in front of the *shulhoyf.* Two Germans carrying guns got out, entered the courtyard with its warren of prayer houses, and asked for the Vilna rabbi. Someone went to get Chaim-Meier Gordon, "a large, tall Jew with a long white beard." He was not the Vilna rabbi, he told the Germans. The first rabbi was in America and the second was dead. Undaunted, the Germans gave Gordon a day to put together a Jewish leadership. The next day, there was one.

The group in Vilna served the same function as Jewish councils elsewhere in German-occupied Europe. In essence, they made the Germans' job easier, though this was not clear in the beginning. At first Jews welcomed the council as a buffer against violence and the actions of the Lithuanian kidnappers. The courtyard of Strashun 6, headquarters of the local Jewish council, was the only place in all of Vilna where a Jew could feel relatively safe, safer even than at home. But not for long.

August 31 was a Sunday, bright and sunny. The Germans, however, were not resting. They were busy sealing off the center of Vilna. The next day, they put up large red posters informing Jews that two of their "cowardly bandits" had shot at German soldiers. Severe measures had been taken in order to prevent similar "acts of terrorism." Jews would be held collectively responsible for "all gestures of hostility vis-à-vis the occupation authorities." To establish "peace and order, Jews had to stay home from 3 P.M. to 10 A.M. the next day. Only workers with the proper papers could be out on the streets."

What happened now was something not even the worst pessimists could have predicted. In the next few days, the Germans carried off thousands of Jews. "Suddenly the terrible news spread about the provocation on Daytsche, Shavler, Mikolayvske, Disner, and other streets," reported Yitzhak. "At night the Jewish population of these streets was led out, we do not know where. Later it became known: to Ponar, where they were shot to death."

"The great provocation" marked the beginning of organized mass murder, a bloodbath that would not come to an end until two years later, with the almost total liquidation of Vilna's Jews. Ponar was a green, wooded area about four miles from Vilna. Before the war, it had been a place where Jewish teachers liked to take their students hiking and camping. The Germans said Ponar was a labor camp; later they spread the story that it was another ghetto. It took some time for the truth about Ponar to sink in, so gruesome were the stories that were going around. Eleven-year-old Jehudit Troyak reported that she had been taken from her home with her family and carried off in covered trucks. "When we got out of the trucks, they took us into a woods between sand hills, and there we waited."

The men had been taken there earlier. The shooting went on all day. Around five o'clock in the afternoon, ten of them were led away and lined up in front of a ditch. She had been blindfolded, but she could still see something. What she saw was a ditch filled with dead people, "a whole mountain." Shots rang out and she was wounded in the hand. Lithuanians were doing the shooting. A woman had dragged her out from the mass grave. Other women, too, had gotten out. They had found shelter with a Lithuanian and next day proceeded to the hospital.

The Germans were masters at keeping Jews off balance, destroying their capacity for action. No sooner had Ponar "passed" than a new calamity struck: a ghetto. Jews were given one day, September 6, to move into the narrow, windy streets of the medieval Jewish quarter that had been designated as their ghetto. "The sad days began of binding packages, of sleepless nights full of restless expectation about the coming days," wrote Yitzhak. "People sit in helpless, painful expectation with their bundles."

GHETTO ONE OR GHETTO TWO?

September 6 rose sunny and warm. Friday. The streets were closed off by Lithuanians. The Poles and Lithuanians were happy. Yet other gentiles, noted Yitzhak, were "standing and taking part in our sorrow."

I go around with bleary eyes among the bundles, see how we are being uprooted overnight from our home.

Soon we have our first view of the move to the ghetto, a picture of the Middle Ages—a gray black mass of people goes harnessed to large bundles. We understand that soon our turn will come. I look at the house in disarray, at the bundles, at the perplexed, desperate people. I see things scattered which were dear to me, which I was accustomed to use. We carry the bundles to the courtyard. On our street a new mass of Jews streams continually to the ghetto. The small number of Jews in our courtyard begin to drag the bundles to the gate. . . . We, too, are carried along with the mass of Jews with their bundles. . . . People fall, bundles scatter. Before me a woman bends under her bundle. From the bundle a thin string of rice keeps pouring over the street.

Like David Rubinowicz on his trip from Krajno to the ghetto of Bodzentyn, Yitzhak walked to his new "home":

I walk burdened and irritated. The Lithuanians drive us on, do not let us rest. I think of nothing: not what I am losing, not what I have just lost, not what is in store for me. I do not see the streets before me, the people passing by. I only feel that I am terribly weary, I feel that an insult, a hurt is burning inside me. Here is the ghetto gate. I feel that I have been robbed, my freedom is being robbed from me, my home, and the familiar Vilna streets I love so much. I have been cut off from all that is dear and precious to me.

The Rudashevskis' new address was Shavler 4. Eleven people in a "dirty and stuffy" room. On the first day in his new surroundings, Yitzhak felt as though he were "in a box. There is no air to breathe." On the second night, three German soldiers burst into their building. "They search, crawl over the bedding with their feet. They look for rings on people's fingers, ransack, make a mess of the slumbering house, and go away without taking anything. Women shout after them: 'Thank you, dear sir, good night.' I do not understand the reason for the thanks—because they have not been robbed?"

Continuing to play their cat-and-mouse game with great skill, the Germans created a second ghetto soon after the first. The ghettos were separated by Niemiecka—German—Street. Ghetto one held around thirty thousand Jews; ghetto two, ten thousand. (Another six thousand Jews were in Lukishki prison awaiting Ponar.) Everyone realized that the two ghettos would not continue to coexist, recalled the poet Sutzkever, "but no one knew which would survive: the first contained more skilled laborers, but the second was better supplied with food." To increase the chances of survival, many families split into two parts, "half in one, half in the other." The Rudashevskis lived in the first.

Yom Kippur is the holiest day in the Jewish calendar. In 1941 it fell on October 1. All day long German storm troopers and Lithuanians kept pouring into the ghetto. "At night things suddenly become turbulent. The people get up. The gate opens. An uproar develops. I look at the courtyard and see them leading away people with bundles. I hear boots pounding on the stairs. Soon, however, things calmed down." The next morning Yitzhak woke up to the terrible news that several thousand people had been taken out of ghetto

one and that ghetto two had been liquidated altogether. "Thus the second ghetto became a snare to
capture thousands of defenseless Jews."

Hard on the heels of the ghetto one and ghetto two
tragedy came the charade with the *shaynen*. In the
ghetto, a job spelled life. But for a job you needed a
special certificate—a *shayne*, in Yiddish—and the wily
executioner made sure that not everyone had one. Every so often the Germans would change the rules of
the *shaynen* game, and each time heads would roll.

As with the creation of the second ghetto and other
Nazi snares, it took a while for Jews to catch on. In
two years' time, there were some dozen and a half
changes: certificates with photos and certificates without; certificates that were white, blue, pink, green, vi-
olet, red, yellow, and in various combinations. The
frequent changes drove everyone crazy.

Yitzhak's father had a job in a munitions storehouse.
He had a white certificate. But in mid-October 1941,
the white certificate became worthless and was super-
seded by yellow, the new color of life. The yellow pass
was valid until March 31, 1942, and granted immunity
to its owner and three family members: a spouse and
two children up to the age of sixteen. Twelve thousand
people could survive on the three thousand certificates
in circulation. The population of ghetto one, however,
was over twenty-seven thousand, which left more than
fifteen thousand to be killed.

Fate suddenly split the people of the ghetto into two
parts. One part possesses the yellow certificate. They
believe in the power of this little piece of paper. It

bestows the right to life. The second part—lost, despairing people—people who sense their doom, and do not know where to go. We do not have a yellow certificate. Our parents are running around like hundreds of others, as though in a fever.

The Jews were desperate and tried everything to get hold of yellow passes. They pleaded with "the chosen ones" to be registered with them. They offered money and gold. They appealed for solidarity in front of the Jewish council building: a yellow pass for all or for none. Girls married and brought their yellow certificate as dowry. People faced impossible choices. Whom to save? "I admit it: I love my mother more than I do my wife," argued one Jew, "but my wife is the mother of my children, and mama is already old." But one has only one mother, argued another, and one can always marry again. Children scoured the streets searching for "parents" with yellow permits, whimpering, "Who doesn't have a child? Who wants to be my father?"

Like everyone else, the Rudashevskis joined the scramble for yellow certificates. Yitzhak desperately envied the people with yellow certificates. "They are headed for life. . . . I, too, would like to leave the accursed ghetto, which is becoming a terrible snare. I wish like them . . . to leave the storm behind me, to save my life."

At this time *maline*—hideout—became a household word. In the turbulent weeks after the Yom Kippur bloodletting of October 1, German "actions" followed one another in rapid succession. Jews buried themselves in their makeshift refuges, which in most cases the Germans and their Lithuanian cohorts had not the least trouble sniffing out. Yitzhak and his family spent many an anxious moment cowering in fright in the hideout built into the warehouses of their courtyard at Shavler 4.

Many people have gathered in the two stories of the hideout. They sneak along like shadows by candlelight around the cold, dank cellar walls. The whole hideout is filled with a restless murmuring. An imprisoned mass of people. Everyone begins to settle down in the corners, on the stairs. Pillows and bundles are spread out on the hard bricks and boards, and people fall asleep. . . . From time to time someone lights a match. By the light I see people lying on the bricks like rags in the dirt. I think: Into what kind of helpless, broken creature can man be transformed? I am at my wit's end. I begin to feel very nauseated. . . .

We are like animals surrounded by the hunter. The hunter on all sides: beneath us, above us, from the sides. Broken locks snap, doors creak, axes, saws. I feel the enemy under the boards on which I am standing. The light of an electric bulb seeps through the cracks. They pound, tear, break. Soon the attack is heard from another side. Suddenly, somewhere upstairs, a child bursts into tears. A desperate groan breaks forth from everyone's lips. We are lost. A desperate attempt to shove sugar into the child's mouth is of no avail. They stop up the child's mouth with pillows. The mother of the child is weeping. People shout in wild terror that the child should be strangled. The child is shouting more loudly, the Lithuanians are pounding more strongly against the walls. However, slowly everything calmed down of itself. We understand that they have left. Later we heard a voice from the other side of the hideout. You are liberated. My heart beat with such joy! I have remained alive!

It was eight o'clock in the evening when Yitzhak crawled out. The next morning he learned that five thousand people had been carried off to Ponar and shot. "The ghetto is full of lamentation. Sobbing, dejected people . . . How dreadful is the dawn!"

One casualty was Yitzhak's friend Benkye Nayer. "He is not to be found!" Yitzhak cried as he combed the ghetto looking for his pal. "I have lost such a good friend," he moaned. "I am constantly thinking about this fine fellow. We miss him now, Benkye Nayer. In the ghetto he always thought about our present condition. He said, 'I shall not go to Ponar.' But he apparently went there after all. I shall always remember you, Benkye! We shall avenge your blood."

At last Yitzhak's mother succeeded in getting a yellow certificate, and he breathed a sigh of relief. The certificate was for a *Schneiderstube* (a tailor shop), which was considered a good place to work. On November 3, a decree sent all yellow-certificate holders to the second ghetto, which had been emptied of Jews in the Yom Kippur action the month before. These were "the saved"; "the drowned" stayed behind to face the merciless "wild Lithuanians" in "the defenseless little streets" on their own. This time the toll was eight thousand, including Yitzhak's grandmother. "We leave her alone in the middle of the street and we run to save ourselves. I shall never forget the two imploring hands and eyes, which begged: 'Take me along!' We left the ghetto."

The purges brought on by the introduction of the yellow *shaynen* were followed, a few months later, by the "Pink Pass Action." The roundup of people without pink certificates took place in December 1941 and claimed another thousand lives, raising the total number of Jews killed since the beginning of the German occupation to 33,500. The ghetto now held about 20,000 Jews, with and without work permits. Most of these would survive until September 1943, when the Nazis closed the book on Jewish Vilna with a final round of murder and deportation.

"OUR WILL TO LIVE"

The Germans created, then shattered, many illusions. The illusion that work passes guaranteed life. The illusion that Ponar was a labor camp or a ghetto. The illusion that a Jewish council would temper Nazi excesses. "The enemy is strong, crafty," observed Yitzhak, "he is exterminating us according to a plan, and we are discouraged." This was the situation at the beginning of 1942.

But for the moment things had settled down; the mood in the ghetto improved. This relative calm is reflected in Yitzhak's diary. In the tailor shop where his mother had found work, Jews even made fun of the Germans and played jokes on them. A German wanted a cap made and was taken to "the best cap maker of Poland." They told the German to bring material, cigarettes, food, and so forth. "Finally they make him a hat which looks like a blintz on him and he is happy as a lark." "They add the blessing, *'Mitn rosh in adome'* ['May your head be hidden in the ground'], and he answers, 'Thank you very much.' . . . They get along well with the Germans." Nevertheless, Yitzhak realized that these stories were "merely wishful thinking," and that people were "actually afraid of the German. However, if it is possible to curse him, to play a trick on him, they do so whenever they can."

All it took was for Franz Murer to poke his cap into the shop for the tricks and the banter to stop dead. Franz Murer was in charge of Jewish affairs in Vilna. With his blond hair, square jaw, and cruel mouth, he resembled the perfect Aryan. When the shout "Here comes Murer" resounded, the streets of the ghetto emptied and everyone raced off to their *malines*. Murer also liked to pop in at the bathhouse to watch the women bathing (he pronounced them too fat). Yitzhak called him "a mad, wild beast," who made Jews crawl around the tables and chairs for his amusement.

Another wild animal was Murer's boss, Hans Hingst. Hingst was responsible for the decrees prohibiting Jewish males from growing mustaches and Jewish women from wearing lipstick and dying their hair, and all Jews from eating foods rich in oil. Hingst was almost bald, had a large, oval face, and the eyes of an administrative killer. He and Murer were responsible for the liquidation of the Jews of Vilna.

Murer and Hingst were no exceptions. Martin Weiss, "the Boss of Ponar," "loved murder as a musician loves his violin." Weiss knew no greater joy than "to strangle a child with his own hands." Hans Kitel, Weiss's successor, once shot a Jew with one hand as he continued to play the piano with the other. Weiss's twenty-three-year-old predecessor, Horst Schweinenberg, found amusement in throwing cakes at mental patients. Done playing, he had them shot.

With men such as these, Jews could never be sure of the ground under their feet. Nevertheless, many thought that those who had weathered the storms of the first half year could save themselves through work. In a sense, the slogan that topped the gate of Auschwitz, *Arbeit macht frei,* "Work Sets You Free," had a certain truth here: Work might not make you free, but it did seem to hold out the best hope for survival. Germany was at war and needed labor. After visiting the ghetto workshops with his class, Yitzhak was struck by "the impression of the power of the will to live. . . . It seems that everything I have seen here was created solely by will."

The quieter times were evident in Yitzhak's daily life. Mature beyond his age, he had taken on many new responsibilities. With both parents working, Yitzhak had become the housekeeper. "I have learned to cook, to wash floors, and on this I spend my days." Best of all, school was reopening. But in mid-September 1942 there was an epidemic, and the school's opening was put off. Yitzhak was bored and could not wait to get back to his lessons. "It is a terrible time when you cannot settle down to some kind of work and you waste your days on nothing." "When in the world will we get back to our studies?" he asked a few days later. "When I used to go to my lessons, I knew how to divide the days, and the days would fly, and now they drag by for me grayly and sadly. Oh, how dreary and sad it is to sit locked up in a ghetto."

School would have to wait, though. On Sunday, September 27, 1942, Yitzhak came down with a light form of jaundice. Racked with fever, a piece of news reached him that struck him "like a clap of thunder: Teacher Gershteyn has died. How beloved and precious he was to me in his proud, pure appearance."

Yitzhak loved his teacher. Jacob Gershteyn was an exceptional human being, with a great love for his profession and utter devotion to his students. He was heir to a tradition in which ordinary teachers were respected and the great ones revered. It is no accident that the spiritual leaders of the Jews are called *rabbis*, "teachers"; a man who spent his days bent over books was considered an ideal husband. And in the misery of the ghetto, Gershteyn had been a light and a hope.

I sensed the tremendous loss: How were we to imagine our dear school, which stood firmly through the years and brought up a new generation, without teacher Gershteyn! How popular teacher Gershteyn was in the school! How everyone who knew him loved his handsome, tall figure, which used to look so beautiful against the background of our school! How beautifully, with what youthfulness he used to go up the school steps, carrying his galoshes and cane in his hands! With what beautiful majesty he used to walk through the school corridors, through the auditorium! A picture of a Yiddish writer was not hanging straight. Teacher Gershteyn is right there, and with what affection he straightens the picture! With what affection did his beautiful eyes shine at a Yiddish word or a Yiddish song! How much he loved his language, his people! And this love, the national pride which he represented, he endeavored to kindle in us. We are his disciples. . . .

The teacher Gershteyn suffered a great deal in the ghetto. He became grayer and grayer, his face darkened. He lived in a class of our school. He could hardly go up the steps, which he used to ascend so cheerfully. He had to stop at every step in his wrinkled coat, which probably served as a pillow for him. . . . Slowly, an old man before his time, he used to walk over the streets of the ghetto, but his head was erect as usual. That is how the best among us suffered in the ghetto. . . . The ghetto was too difficult for Gershteyn, and he did not survive it. I thought a long, long time about our teacher Gershteyn. He stands before my eyes. He appears so beautifully, so freshly before me from the midst of our dreary life. Forever and ever will we remember you as our dear friend, the image of your proud figure will remind us of something that is precious and dear. What you have given us of yourself will always flourish among us.

Gershteyn was buried on Monday, September 27, 1942. A month later Yitzhak presented his tribute to Gershteyn in public. He first read it in class, and again at a special memorial service held that evening in the ghetto theater. There were many people. He was nervous. "It seemed very strange to me: the artists, the speakers make room for me and arrange with me the order of the speeches. I feel my cheeks burning." After many "fine, well-rounded speeches" extolling the character of the departed teacher and bemoaning his irreplaceability, it was his turn. Standing up on stage, Yitzhak repeated the thoughts he had written in his diary the day he had learned of his teacher's death.

> The edginess which filled me until now disappears. I feel quite free. I make an effort to read loudly, with expression. The moments fly by swift as an arrow: "To me, teacher Gershteyn will always be unique, beautiful, and festive." And finally I read the conclusion, "The name Jacob Gershteyn will always flourish among us, and remind us of the dearest and the best." I take my seat. I feel myself blushing again. I felt such exalted [emotions] as I was reading. As I was reading I sensed my teacher Gershteyn in the depths of my being. At night we go home in a group. They tell me I read well, a fine essay. While lying in bed my cheeks still burned. . . . I shall never forget that evening, sitting at the dais, my reading, just as I shall never forget my teacher Gershteyn.

Around the time of Gershteyn's death, another "oak rooted in Jewish Vilna" fell. His name was Dr. Joseph

Heller, also a teacher. His son, Gabik Heller, was one of Yitzhak's best friends and a Pioneer. The two spent a lot of time together. Gabik had a job as a volunteer in the ghetto library and seldom got enough to eat. His father had a heart condition and died on the evening of November 7, 1942. "I sensed how much misfortune inheres in this world. I feel great pity for Gabik, for his mother. How terrible is the lot of these quiet, lonely people! How honestly, how poorly did they live, how quiet and refined they were! How hard will it now be for Gabik, how he loved his father! Gabik's misfortune struck deep into my heart."

"I SHALL LIVE WITH TOMORROW, NOT WITH TODAY"

What kept Yitzhak going was his love of learning. A classroom in winter may be as cold as the house, "but while studying it somehow becomes warmer." Looking around him, he saw people turned into machines whose only thought was of survival. "I long for the studies which sustain us in the ghetto," he wrote. "Without them we become lazier and more negligent." "I need to study," he declared in January 1943. "My determination to study has developed into something like defiance of the present, which hates to study, loves to work, to drudge. No, I decided. I shall live with to-morrow, not with today. And if for every one hundred ghetto children of my age ten can study, I must be among the fortunate ones. I must take advantage of this. Studying has become even more precious to me than before."

Besides school, Yitzhak had "the club." The club was his favorite place. It was located in a clean and well-lighted space where students and other young people came to do their homework, learn a trade, discuss literature, history, mathematics, work on plays, or simply relax. Teachers gave lectures and organized discussions on topics ranging from the psychology of the ghetto child to the evolution of capitalism, and tried to create the illusion of normal life, recalled Abraham Sutzkever, himself a regular contributor to club life. "They desperately wanted to keep the children uncorrupted and to make them into dignified, confident people capable of dealing with the future after liberation."

The club opened in October 1942. "We have groups for literature, natural science. After leaving class at seven thirty, I go immediately to the club. It is gay there. We have a good time and return home evenings in a large crowd." Bursting with pride, Yitzhak related the happenings at the "great club festival" held in the evening of Saturday, January 9, 1943. On the freshly painted wall of the premises hung a copy of *Within Walls, Yet Young,* the newspaper Yitzhak had helped edit:

A splendid newspaper. The articles are in the form of walls and a street leading to the ghetto gate. The whole appearance of the paper symbolizes the masthead, and the content of the articles and poems also prove the correctness of the newspaper headline [masthead]. A beautiful bulletin gives an account of the work that has been done.

The dramatic performances went splendidly, and after the show, the producers and performers hung around "until half past two, intoxicated with youthful joy." "We are young," exulted Yitzhak, "the . . . hall is saturated with youthful joy and work. Our spirit, which we bear proudly within the ghetto walls, will be the most beautiful gift to the newly rising future. Long live youth!—the progress of our people."

It was at the club that Yitzhak spent his happiest day in the ghetto, December 11, 1942. That evening there was a club party in the kitchen of the Jewish council building at Rudnitski 6. The members of the club managed to get hold of 220 pounds of potatoes and make a baked pudding. The party started at nine.

People are already sitting at the tables. Many, many guests came. And here we sit crowded together. I look around at the crowd, all of our kind teachers, friends, intimates. It is so cozy, so warm, so pleasant. This evening we demonstrated what we are and what we can accomplish. Club members came with songs, recitations. Until late into the night we sang with the adults songs which tell about youthfulness and hope. . . . We sat at the meager tables and ate baked pudding and coffee, and we were so happy, so happy.

Yitzhak was a busy person. One of his projects was a history of courtyard Shavler 4, the housing complex that was his home in the ghetto. In November a Jewish history circle formed. "We resolved to learn, to study Jewish history, and to deal with the problems in Jewish history that interest us and can have current application, especially most recent Jewish history." Hours later he was "picked to serve on the executive of the literary circle," which intended "to collect material for folklore. With such activity," he concluded, "you do not feel the cold." And the load kept getting bigger. "Lately I have a pile of work from school and the club," he wrote on Monday, November 23, 1942.

> We spend whole days on historical books. We are preparing various reports and [mock] trials. In addition, I am the person responsible for the circle of creative writing in the club, under the direction of the poet Sutzkever, and I have to be in constant contact with him. . . . I am burdened by piles of reports in Yiddish, in history. And everything comes up at the same time. Every evening I go to the club as usual, visit the history circles, the nature circle, the literary one.

For the project on the history of courtyard Shavler 4, the members of the history circle had prepared questionnaires for the residents to fill out about life under Polish, Soviet, and German rule.

> The residents answer in different ways. Everywhere, however, the same sad ghetto song: property, certificates, hideouts, the abandonment of things, the abandonment of relatives. I got a taste of the historian's task. I sit at the table and ask questions and record the greatest sufferings with cold objectivity. I write, I

probe into details, and I do not realize at all that I am
probing into wounds, and the one who answers me—
indifferent to it: two sons and a husband taken—the
sons Monday, the husband Thursday. . . . And this horror, this tragedy is formulated by me in three words,
coldly and dryly. I become absorbed in thought, and
the words stare out of the paper crimson with blood.

Some of the people Yitzhak interviewed for the ghetto
history project poured their hearts out—"Write, write,
children. It is good this way"—while others were "terribly cautious and exceptionally diplomatic," carefully
weighing and measuring every word. "If we ask them
where they lived before the ghetto, they do not answer.
If you ask them in which unit they work, they do not
answer. They regard us as people whose job it is to levy
taxes." Having been rebuked for "probing into another
person's wounds," Yitzhak reflected: "She is right, but
I am not at fault either, because I consider that everything should be recorded and noted down, even the
most gory, because everything will be taken into account."

After a meeting and talk with the poet Sutzkever on
November 2, the literary group decided to create sec-
tions dealing with Yiddish poetry and ghetto folklore.
The latter interested Yitzhak very much. "In the
ghetto dozens of sayings, ghetto curses and ghetto
blessings, are created before our eyes . . . even songs,
jokes, and stories which already sound like legends. I
feel that I shall participate zealously in this little circle,
because the ghetto folklore . . . which is scattered over

the little streets, must be collected and cherished as a treasure for the future."

Yitzhak kept so busy that he even forgot his own birthday. It was only after December 10, 1942, had already passed that it dawned on him that he had turned fifteen. "You hardly realize how time flies," he reflected. "It, the time, runs ahead unnoticed and presently we realize, as I did today, for example, and discover that days and months go by, that the ghetto is not a painful, squirming moment of a dream which constantly disappears, but is a large swamp in which we lose our days and weeks."

His fifteenth birthday was a time for taking stock, for making resolutions.

> I made up my mind not to trifle my time away in the ghetto on nothing, and I feel somehow happy that I can study, read, develop myself, and see that time does not stand still as long as I progress normally with it. In my daily ghetto life, it seems to me that I live normally but often I have deep qualms. Surely I could have lived better. Must I day in day out see the walled-up ghetto gate, must I in the best years see only the one little street, the few stuffy courtyards? . . . I wish to shout to time to linger, not to run. I wish to recapture my past year and keep it for later, for the new life. My second feeling today is that of strength and hope. I do not feel the slightest despair. Today I became fifteen years of age, and I live confident in the future. I am not conflicted about it and see before me sun and sun and sun.

Three days later the ghetto celebrated the circulation of the hundred thousandth book from the ghetto library.

"The reading of books in the ghetto is the greatest pleasure for me," wrote Yitzhak on that occasion. "The book unites us with the future, the book unites us with the world. The circulation of the hundred thousandth book is a great achievement for the ghetto, and the ghetto has the right to be proud of it."

HEROD ON TRIAL

Some of those 100,000 books had been checked out by Yitzhak to prepare for the public trial against Herod, a school assignment. "We have a court, prosecutor, defense counsel, defendant, and a whole succession of persons from history who serve as witnesses," reported Yitzhak on November 11, 1942. "Now the hardest task is in store for me—to work out the indictment and to prepare a series of questions for the witnesses on behalf of the prosecution. You have to study [the Jewish historians] Graetz, Dubnow, and others."

A large crowd consisting of club members and their guests was on hand the evening the trial took place, Monday, December 21, 1942.

> I made the first speech for the prosecution. . . . I accused Herod of a policy of ambiguity, of playing the role of a Roman agent, of introducing into the land Roman customs which were hostile and foreign to Jewish spirituality. I accused him of murdering the people. The defense showed Herod's positive deeds, explained that Herod had lived in a tempestuous time, that his behavior was contrary to his will, and that

many of his deeds were for the benefit of the Jewish people.

After each side had had its say, "the court selected a committee of experts consisting of teachers and historians, which had to answer the question of whether Herod's deeds were in the interest of the people. A great discussion opened among the adults and this was the most interesting part." The committee ruled that Herod was guilty. Yitzhak was satisfied.

In a sense, the real man on the stand was not Herod but ghetto chief Jacob Gens. When the director of the school, Leyb Turbovitsh, defended Herod on the ground that "the revolt against Rome would have hastened the catastrophe," he was defending Gens and his policy of trying to save lives through work. "The basis for the existence of the ghetto," Gens stated on coming to power in July 1942, "is Labor, Discipline, and Order." The head of Vilna's Jewish council publicly declared that he would sacrifice 400 to save 1,000, for as many Jews as possible had to survive, "regardless of our good name and personal experience."

At the beginning of January 1943, Yitzhak received his grades. "I have A's in Yiddish, Jewish history, history, and biology. I have B's in mathematics, Hebrew, drawing, and physics; in Latin, German, C's." "My grades could perhaps have been better," he commented, "but even those mentioned above are proof that my time is not being frittered away."

In March 1943, Yitzhak mused: "I often reflect, this is supposedly the ghetto, yet I have such a rich life of intellectual work: I study, I read, I visit club circles. Time runs by so quickly and there is so much work to be done, lectures, social gatherings. I often forget that I am in the ghetto."

What was true for Yitzhak individually held for the ghetto as a whole: Its absorption in cultural pursuits was so complete as to border on obsession. There were symphony and theater performances, art exhibits, lectures, discussion circles, and literary contests with prizes. There was a conservatory and a "university" with various faculties.

On the first anniversary of the ghetto theater (January 15, 1943), Jewish council head Jacob Gens said the theater strived

> to give man the opportunity to free himself from the ghetto for several hours, and this we achieved. We are passing through dark and difficult days. Our bodies are in the ghetto, but our spirit has not been enslaved. . . . Before the first concert it was said that concerts should not be held in graveyards. True, the statement is true, but all of life is now a graveyard. Our hands must not falter. We must be strong in body and soul.

THE RUINS ARE WEEPING

But no matter how high the wall of words, music, and art Jews built for themselves, the wall around the ghetto was higher. All the books in the world could not shield Yitzhak or any other ghetto dwellers from its misery. In the fall of 1942, a part of the ghetto was torn down. Yitzhak saw that as a symbol of their lives.

> How much tragedy and anguish is mirrored in every shattered brick, in every dark crack, in every bit of plaster with a piece of wallpaper. . . . Here, here, here on the black walls is inscribed in blood and tears all our tragedy and pain. As I look at the ruins an uncanny feeling comes over me to see how Jews putter around there. I, too, crawl between the bricks, pieces of wallpaper, tiles, and it seems to me a lamentation ascends from the black crevices, from the stale holes. It seems to me that the ruins are weeping and importuning as though lives were hidden here. . . . I shudder. Like a ghost, the bare ruin stands before the ghetto and importunes and haunts and opens one's wounds. . . . And everyone is glad to see it crashing and becoming smaller and smaller.

"There is so much injustice evident among us Jews in the ghetto," lamented Yitzhak, "so much that is not right, so much that is disgusting. People have somehow become cheap." "How terribly sad!" he exclaimed after witnessing the beating of a woman caught stealing food from a bakery. "People are grabbing morsels from each other's mouths. I am overcome with pity for the hungry woman, how she is being insulted with the dirtiest words, how they beat her. I think: What peculiarly ugly things occur in the ghetto! On the one hand, the ugliness of stealing a pot of food, and on the other to strike a woman crudely in the face because she is probably hungry."

Most people thought only of themselves. What really mattered, noted Yitzhak, was pull—*pleytses*—that is, "*strong* shoulders." While patiently waiting his turn at the butcher shop, ration card in hand, "people with briefcases," Jewish policemen, and other privileged persons swept past him and got VIP treatment. "During the distribution, the butcher throws the piece of meat to the person in line as if he were doing him a favor, exploiting a child, a person who is less vituperative, by giving him the worst." To those who have *pleytses,* however, the butcher "extends his sweet, wheedling face to them in such a disgusting manner, cuts out a piece of thick, white fat for them," and all this while a "crowd of frozen women stands in line, hushed, wrathful, devouring the meat with their eyes" and "remain silent as they watch one person receive the fat and the second bones. People are already used to it."

The ghetto of Vilna had a Jewish police. While many Jews may have congratulated themselves on this, expecting Jews to curb the German potential for harm, Yitzhak suspected otherwise. "They are supposed to keep order in the ghetto," he remarked. "In time, however, they become a caste which helps the oppressors with their work. With the help of the Jewish police, the Gestapo accomplished many things in the course of time. The Jewish police help to grasp their brothers by the throat, they help to trip up their brothers."

"Our police dressed up in their new hats," Yitzhak wrote on November 1, 1942.

Here one of them is passing—my blood boils—in a leather overcoat, with an insolent air, his officer's hat askew. Its peak shines in the sun. The cord of his hat drops over his chin, he clicks his shiny boots. Satiated, gorged with food, he struts proudly like an officer, delights—the snake—in such a life, and plays his comedy. This is the source of all my anger against them, that they are playing a comedy with their own tragedy.

On November 8, 1942, he saw the burial of a Jewish policeman, who was fussed over like a prince of the realm, "a victim to his duty." "The cantor sang, a rabbi spoke, representatives of the work units and leaders of the police." His colleagues, decked out in their leather overcoats, boots, green round hats with glossy peaks and Stars of David, filed past the coffin on which lay the deceased's police hat and his stripe. "At the sides firemen with torches: impressive, solemn, 'a hero' has fallen. The foolish crowd ambles up and presses forward to look on. I feel sad at heart."

Yet Yitzhak knew that the slain policeman and those who had sent him off with full honors were victims themselves. Take the gatekeeper Levas. It was Levas's job to make sure that Jews who worked outside the ghetto did not smuggle in goods, and he performed this duty like a man possessed. He thought nothing of administering twenty-five lashes to a boy who had brought food into the ghetto for his family. "Four policemen," reported Yitzhak, "held him and Levas himself, the commander of the gatekeepers, beat him mercilessly, so murderously. The little breadwinner was brought home badly flogged." Then, on January 1, 1943, Levas got married with all the pomp due a gate-keeper. Yitzhak:

> The ghetto hates Levas. Perhaps Levas is compelled to beat people, but the people must hate the one who beats and insults them at the gate every day. The dejected, embittered ghetto Jew cannot figure out that Levas was perhaps beating him against his will; the Jew at the gate feels the blow of his knout, and he feels hatred to Levas as a traitor. And today, on the day of Levas's magnificent wedding, the people curse him.

"LET US NOT BE LED LIKE SHEEP TO THE SLAUGHTER"

While the Jews of Vilna were doing their best to stay alive, the Germans continued to kill. Picking their spots, they gradually emptied out the smaller provincial ghettos. The victims of five such ghettos, five thousand Jews, were brought first to Vilna, whence they would be taken to the ghetto of Kovno, or so they had been told. But on Sunday, April 4, 1943, "at three o'clock the streets in the ghetto were closed off," and they were taken out to Ponar. "It has begun again," wrote Yitzhak. "Again there hovers over the little Vilna ghetto streets the nightmare of Ponar."

But this time, he announced, the Jews were ready to resist. "We believe in our own strength. We are ready at any moment." Almost two years had passed since

Yitzhak had bitten his lips observing the helplessness of the Jews, their fragmentation, their passivity—"dying passively like sheep." He had been ashamed that thousands of Jews were letting themselves be carried off, with the rest scampering to save their own lives "and not to attempt to defend themselves."

Yitzhak was not alone in his anger and humiliation. He had just turned fourteen when an event took place that he must have known about. On January 1, 1942, a young poet named Abba Kovner, standing in a public soup kitchen, read the manifesto "Let Us Not Be Led like Sheep to the Slaughter," which exhorted Jewish youth "to rise up with arms" until "their last breath" against the murderers. Three weeks later, the F.P.O., or United Partisan Organization, was founded, with a ghetto revolt as its goal. The F.P.O. was the first Jewish organization to prepare for armed resistance.

In the time still left before the liquidation of the ghetto, the question of passivity versus resistance, of not being led "like sheep to the slaughter," became a lively topic of discussion. In "the last two weeks new elements generally have been added to my life," announced Yitzhak toward the end of February 1943. They had started a cell devoted to resistance. "The future will require dedicated people who will have to guide the masses toward great renewal. Our first condition for such a task is discipline and conspiracy. For the first time I now sensed what it means to work in secret."

To what extent Yitzhak was personally involved in partisan activities other than discussion we do not know. But Abraham Sutzkever, in his book about the Vilna ghetto, speaks of "young Rudashevski," who can be no other than Yitzhak. In the winter of 1942, the poet had a job transporting clothing collected from Vilna residents. The caps, boots, coats, and so forth were destined for the Russian front. At the time, a group of Soviet prisoners of war—officers and their families—were interned in two guarded houses outside the ghetto. Instead of taking the looted materials to the German depot, Sutzkever and "young Rudashevski" managed to divert part of it to the Russians. This they kept up for a week.

Yitzhak may well have inspired Sutzkever's poem "The Last Jew of the Maline," which begins:

> Where are you going, through wind and night,
> Your eyes glowing with murder, rage,
> And your look afire with hate?
> I am going where my feet carry me,
> My murdered and bleeding flesh burns me,
> Now I am the last Jew,
> The Jew of the Maline.

"WE MAY BE FATED FOR THE WORST"

Purim commemorates the Jews' deliverance from destruction at the hands of the Persian prime minister Haman. On Sunday, March 21, 1943, there was a Purim party at the club. "We were in the mood for

Purim, so let it be Purim." (Yitzhak and company were not particularly religious.) Everybody had a good time. "We laughed our fill and went to sleep. We are waiting for the real Purim. Next year we shall eat Hitler-taschen," Yitzhak punned. (*Hamantaschen* are small, triangular-shaped pastries filled with a combination of poppy seeds and honey or prunes, nuts, and citrus fruits traditionally eaten during Purim.)

Less than three weeks later, Yitzhak seems to have stopped writing. His final diary entry is dated April 7, 1943. On the fifth, five thousand provincial Jews were rounded up and shot at Ponar. "The ghetto was deeply shaken, as though struck by thunder." Horrific scenes fill the final entries of his diary: railroad tracks littered with corpses, children running away from home to escape the terrible mood, a Jew running through the street, his fur coat covered with lime, police digging the dead Jews out of Ponar's lime pits, despondent teachers, schools closed . . .

> In the evening I went out into the streets. . . . It becomes darker and darker. Suddenly a clap of thunder, a flash of lightning and it begins to rain. . . . The rain lashes with anger, as though it wished to flush everything out of the world."

The final liquidation of the ghetto took place on September 23 and 24, 1943. The women and the children were "disposed of" in Maidanek, the death camp located near Lublin, Poland. Men capable of working were sent to camps in Estonia, north of Lithuania, where the great majority of them died.

Yitzhak's diary was found shortly after Vilna's liberation by Soviet troops in the summer of 1944. The finder was his cousin, Sore Voloshin, who had spent the final weeks with him in hiding. Sore, who managed to get away and join the partisans, reported that Yitzhak just could not take it anymore. On September 23, she testified, the Rudashevskis moved into a *maline* with her family. Of Yitzhak's last weeks, she remembered only this: "He reached a state of apathy, and I do not recall his participating in any discussion during the period of liquidation." "Toward the end," she recalled, "raids and liquidations went on all the time; day in, day out, week after week, groups of people perished in Ponar, and this grieved him deeply."

The final words of the diary: "We may be fated for the worst."

A Jew in departing / A Jew in arriving
A Jew in arising / A Jew in sitting
A Jew in walking / A Jew in standing
A Jew in thought / A Jew in deeds
A Jew in trouble / A Jew in joy
A Jew in speech / A Jew in silence
A Jew in drinking / A Jew in eating
A Jew in business / A Jew in studying
A Jew in shoes / A Jew in clothing
A Jew in hatred / A Jew in love
A Jew in God / A Jew in people
A Jew in life / A Jew in death
A Jew in heaven / A Jew on earth
A Jew you were born / A Jew you will die.

Photo courtesy of Film and Photo Archives Department, Yad Vashem

CHAPTER 3

Moshe Flinker

"My Name Is Harry"

Moshe Ze'ev Flinker was born in The Hague on October 9, 1926. His father, Eliezer Noah Flinker, a Polish Jew, had come to Holland before Moshe's birth and done well for himself. He was blessed with a good business and many children, five girls and two boys. Moshe was the older boy. When the Nazis invaded Holland, on May 10, 1940, he was thirteen years old and preparing to follow in his father's footsteps, studying business.

In Holland, the Germans took their time getting started on their Jewish agenda. One early decree, however, hit the Flinkers hard. This was the prohibition of ritual slaughter, the killing of animals according to Jewish dietary laws. The Flinkers were Orthodox Jews who would eat only kosher food. The pace of persecution picked up in 1941. In August, Moshe started attending a Jewish school, as Jewish children were no longer permitted to sit next to Aryans. Nine months later he wore the yellow "Badge of Shame." By July, it took him an hour and a half to get to school: His bicycle had become Nazi property, and Jews were no longer allowed to ride the streetcar.

The first transport of Jews left the Netherlands on July 15, 1942. From then on the trains ran like clockwork, smoothly, furiously, until, a year and a half later, practically the only Jews left in the country were those in hiding, such as the Franks in Amsterdam.

On August 2, a high-ranking Nazi gave a speech blasting the Jews as Germany's worst enemy and prophesied that they would be dispatched to the east "as poor and covered with lice" as they had come west. "A hard fate will be theirs," the German official warned. The speech was widely quoted in the Dutch press, and Jews took note. Right after, the Flinkers decided to "go underground," but not in Holland. Casting about for ways to move his family out of danger, Mr. Flinker settled on Belgium, where they were going to try to "pass," to hide in plain sight by pretending to be gentiles. From there they hoped to have a better chance of going on to Vichy France (that part left unoccupied by the Nazis) or to neutral Switzerland. A month later they were in Belgium.

It was no small feat for nine people to cross the border and arrange a place to stay. But Moshe's father had money and connections, and eventually the Flinker family wound up in Schaarbeek, a suburb of Brussels. Here they did not feel as afraid as in Holland, "because no one (except a few Jewish friends) knew us," wrote Moshe. "So we ventured out into the streets without wearing our Jewish badge and did other things forbidden to Jews." One of these was to register themselves at Brussels city hall as Dutch nationals. "My mother was very afraid of this because she thought that the Brussels municipality was connected with the Germans, and that when we came to register, some policemen would be waiting for us and they would take us as they take off other Jews." But since registration would enable them to obtain identity cards and food ration coupons, they took the chance, and on September 9 received the documents allowing them to stay for three months. From this Moshe concluded that "there is no connection between the municipal office for foreigners and the Germans," though he did not exclude the possibility that the fifty thousand francs his father had paid out had had something to do with it.

It is ironic that the Flinkers, who were the most devout Jews discussed in this book, were the only ones who had to pretend, daily, that they were not Jews at all. Moshe was well aware of the ambiguity of their situation, and that of Jews in the new racial order generally, as is clear from the following, perhaps imaginary, dialogue; it appears in the back of his diary and is undated.

"You shouldn't carry a Hebrew Bible so openly."

"Why not, sir?"

"Because they can see—for there are Germans everywhere—that you are a Jew."

"I beg your pardon, sir. I am not a Jew."

"What are you then?"

"I am Dutch."

"You can be Dutch and still be a Jew."

"I am Protestant."

"But you can be a Protestant and still be a Jew."

"But sir, you asked me if I am a Jew, and I answered that I was not a Jew. You then asked me what I am, and I replied that I am Dutch and a Protestant. Despite this, you retorted that this does not prevent me from being a Jew. So, what answer did you expect when you asked me if I am a Jew? Really! Sir, one can be all these and a Jew at the same time."

Evidently Brussels remained a dangerous place for the Flinkers, and Moshe's mother kept urging her husband to continue on to Switzerland. Mr. Flinker, however, thought it better to remain in Belgium for the time being. When friends of theirs were caught trying to enter Switzerland illegally, the decision stood.

"A JEW YOU WILL DIE"

Moshe's diary reads like a book from the Old Testament. "We are in a very bad situation," Moshe declared in a tone-setting paragraph at the beginning of the diary.

Our sufferings have by far exceeded our wrongdoings. What other purpose could the Lord have in allowing such things to befall us? I feel certain that further troubles will not bring any Jew back to the paths of righteousness; on the contrary, I think that upon

experiencing such great anguish they will think that
there is no God at all in the universe, because had
there been a God, He would not have let such things
happen to His people. I have heard this said many
times already—and indeed, what can God intend by all
these calamities that are happening to us in this terrible
period? It seems to me that the time has come for our
redemption, or rather, that we are more or less worthy
of being redeemed.

Yitzhak Rudashevski had communism; Moshe had
God, the Jewish God, whom he loved with all his being. Every page of his diary is a Jewish page, from the
dating by the Hebrew calendar and the mournful
prayers that close many of the entries, to the classical
Hebrew he used to express himself. He believed he was
living in exile, homeless, that his true country was "the
Holy Land, the Land of Israel," from which Jews had
been expelled two thousand years earlier. He was convinced that only God could end their exile, and expected a divine redeemer, a messiah, to lead them to
the promised land. "Obviously my outlook is a religious one," he remarked at one point. "I hope to be
excused for this, for had I not religion, I would never
find any answer at all to the problems that confront
me." A poem of his said it best.

> A Jew in departing / A Jew in arriving
> A Jew in arising / A Jew in sitting
> A Jew in walking / A Jew in standing
> A Jew in thought / A Jew in deeds

A Jew in trouble / A Jew in joy
A Jew in speech / A Jew in silence
A Jew in drinking / A Jew in eating
A Jew in business / A Jew in studying
A Jew in shoes / A Jew in clothing
A Jew in hatred / A Jew in love
A Jew in God / A Jew in people
A Jew in life / A Jew in death
A Jew in heaven / A Jew on earth
A Jew you were born / A Jew you will die.

Moshe believed the Jews were God's chosen people and interpreted everything in light of God's will. He believed that only God could solve the so-called Jewish Question and end Jewish suffering.

"WHAT CAN GOD INTEND?"

One question occupied Moshe more than any other: "What can God intend by all these calamities that are happening to us in this terrible period?"

Moshe decided that what was happening to the Jews of his generation was not "a mere link in a long chain of suffering" but something different, and in order to find the difference, he resolved to compare the sufferings of Jews of his day with those of earlier times. He approached the question from many angles. The first difference he found was that "in former times the persecutions were always localized. In one place Jews were badly treated, while in another they lived in peace and quiet." In the past, moreover, Jews had been able to avoid death through conversion, but for the Germans it was enough "that we are JEWS. The fact that we are born Jews is sufficient to explain and justify everything." The second and more important difference he found was that now it was possible to destroy all Jews "without swords or weapons" because "everything is highly organized. . . . And why can they now organize everything in a manner not previously possible?" Moshe continued. "The reason is . . . that with the Germans everything is official, everything is done according to the law. The law condemns us," he asserted. "Just as there is a law against stealing, so there is a law to persecute the Jews."

Firm believer though he was, Moshe still had to answer his most basic question: "Why does the Lord not prevent this, or, on the other hand, why does He permit our tormentors to persecute us?" He could only answer this by believing that Jews were being punished because of their sins. In what way they had sinned, he did not make clear; all he knew was that Jews had suffered more than was necessary to deserve redemption, that time was short and the enemy ruthless.

To Moshe, all roads led to God and only God could bring real salvation. Never mind the Allies. Their victories could bring only partial relief at best, for the kind of rescue Moshe had in mind lay beyond the powers of human beings. Being Orthodox, Moshe fully expected God to intervene directly or through the Messiah. This semidivine messenger would defeat the enemies of the Jews and lead them into the Holy Land, where they would find peace and live happily ever after.

In Moshe's eyes, the very magnitude of the catastrophe was proof that deliverance was at hand, "not merely a relief from suffering as has occurred many times during our exile, but *the* salvation. . . ." It was not the end of the war itself that would bring this about. It was not Germany or the Allies, but God, the Lord of Israel. Salvation, Moshe declared, "will come only when the whole world, and especially the Jews, gives up all hope for a victory by the Allies. Then will the Lord have mercy on us, and His light shall shine upon us, and His salvation will come." The greater the suffering, the more likely and the speedier the redemption.

"The Jews seem so sure that England is stronger than Germany and that she will win," Moshe reflected on December 7, 1942. "The real reason they think this way is because if the Germans win we shall not be permitted to live. But such a reason is no proof that one side or the other will win. Whoever wins is no longer important to me. The main thing is that we Jews will be redeemed and rescued from the troubles of our times." Indeed, he thought that a German victory would hasten Jewish salvation—"the greater her triumph, the greater her fall," he wrote in February 1943.

That, in my opinion, is the only way that salvation will come. . . . And now I understand the feeling of joy I felt when I heard of German victories, and my hatred for England, America, and their Allies. Then I felt, and now I know, that the way to redemption will not be measured by England's victories but by Germany's. For then shall we be saved by the Lord Himself and our two-thousand-year-old exile will come to an end.

Since Moshe thought salvation could come only from God, all his attention was on sin, on religious acts, and on signs of divine favor. Perhaps he felt that only if the situation of Jews was completely hopeless would God be moved to come to the rescue. Allied victories, then, were not even desirable, for they merely postponed that glorious day. When he learned of Russian military successes against the German Army in the east, he was at first happy, seeing in them a sign that God had not forgotten the Jews. But then he realized that no matter what, Jews were "still in exile and all that has happened was for nothing—only part of a long chain of pain has now passed, and before us is another very long chain and the end is not yet in sight. . . . It is not yet time for joy."

Nor was Moshe prepared to concede the Allies the moral high ground. They "who regard themselves as privileged, good, and superior, are really not a whit better than Germany. It is only through them that such a disaster could have befallen us. Cruel Russia, for instance, has already forgotten the many myriads of Jews murdered under its rule, most of whom lost their lives by Russia's intention. Through this war which is desolating her, she is getting what she deserves."

When, early in 1943, Tripoli, on the north coast of Africa, was captured by the British, Moshe's father believed that the end was near and was ecstatic. "As I listened to my father, I thought to myself: 'Is their defeat really near? Is our people's salvation approaching?' And a voice within me answered: 'No! No! Judah will not be saved by the English or any other nation.' " The war, he believed, would end "with the downfall of most of the world because all have tortured our people."

Nevertheless, as time passed, Moshe grew increasingly anxious. Would this war really bring the end of exile or was it only the next "link in a long chain of anguish?" He reminded God that He had a covenant with Jews, and that when Jews were mocked His own honor was at stake. Take pity, he implored. "If not now, when wilt Thou help Thy chosen people, O Lord? Wilt Thou let them die in the cold of Russia?"

Why was God waiting? Maybe, Moshe wondered in June 1943, Jews had not yet been saved because countries like the United States and England had "not committed enough sins to blacken their names completely." But with the Allies pounding German and Italian cities, that was no longer a problem. "Now, when England and America every day drop bombs on defenseless towns, on women, children, and the aged, their list of sins must be getting longer and longer." One month later things looked even more "hopeful." "England and America continue bombing German cities. In my opinion, nothing is to be hoped for from these bombings except that the merit of England and America will diminish. Maybe through the lack of merit of the Allies our redemption will come? Perhaps?"

Religious Jews believe that merit is obtained by freely choosing to obey God's commandments and performing other good deeds. The rewards of performing "meritorious works" can extend to other people including one's family, city, or even country. Merit acquired by past generations can be stored up and benefit the descendants, and can speed up redemption. (The reverse holds for sin and sinners.)

Moshe kept a close watch for signs pointing to salvation, seeing even in the casual remark of a worker an omen announcing better times. When the war started, the man who used to pick up the laundry at the Flinkers' house suddenly had more customers than he could handle. One day he came to the house and Moshe asked him to come back later. "He said to me: 'I really do not have to come back. We have enough customers, but I shall fulfill your request, for after this time another period will come.' " From this Moshe extracted an important moral: "And if the man said this of laundry, then it is surely true concerning the words of the Bible and other things that I revered in peacetime."

"I shall never stop hoping," wrote Moshe in July 1943, "because the moment I stop hoping I shall cease to exist. All I have is hope; my entire being depends on it. And at the same time I have nothing. What will these useless hopes bring me? I don't know what to do."

Moshe never lost faith. Faith, he affirmed on May 25, 1943, is indestructible, an inexhaustible source of strength, "an inner sacred belief in comparison to which all external reality is negligible," "the holiest thing in the world; faith explains and defines all we ought to be, how we ought to conduct ourselves, and what we ought to believe. All this is included in our sacred word 'faith.' . . . Crowning everything is our faith in the God of our forefathers, the eternal God, our Lord, the Lord of Israel, who has guided and protected us this far, through valleys deep as Sheol [hell], over many a hazardous precipice and through the most terrifying fiery trails. We shall never abandon our faith lest we abandon ourselves; our faith will accompany us forever, until by its strength we shall win. . . ."

There came a time when Moshe faced the supreme test of faith. Why did his friend Yonah Yeret have to be killed? When Moshe heard that Yonah had died trying to cross the Dutch-Belgian border, his "heart stopped." He could not believe "that such a good boy, one who seemed to have the Divine Presence always hovering over him," was no longer living. "This is surely not a thing that the Lord would permit." If Yonah had been murdered, Moshe was certain that "the time has really come" for God to take his revenge on "those evil Germans" and to bring about the salvation of the Jews.

SHAME

Officially registered at city hall and fitted out with an identity card, Moshe was able to move about freely. On December 13, 1942, he went to the movies with one of his sisters. Moshe did not really care for movies. No doubt he considered it a frivolous way to spend one's time. In The Hague, he explained, he had hardly ever gone, but when the Germans started showing anti-Semitic films, he was curious. There, however, the cinema had been off-limits to Jews. In Brussels, on the other hand, Moshe was registered as a foreigner and his identity card was not stamped with the telltale *J* for Jew, and so he went.

The film he saw that afternoon was *Jew Süss,* a favorite of Joseph Goebbels, the Nazi Minister of Propaganda. Goebbels considered *Jew Süss* a fine example of inflammatory anti-Semitism masquerading as entertainment. Loosely based on a novel by Lion Feuchtwanger, *Jew Süss* was the story of an eighteenth-century "court Jew," Joseph Süss Oppenheimer, who becomes the financial adviser to Duke Charles Alexander of Württemberg.

The Jew Süss, portrayed in the film as a leering, ruthless, bloodsucking pimp and seducer, is only interested in enriching himself. His hidden agenda is to use his power to overturn the law banning Jews from living in the city of Stuttgart. The duke, a lecherous spendthrift, turns out to be no match for the cunning, cosmopolitan Jew. The Jew Süss succeeds in having the law changed, and his success, the film stresses, is ruinous for the German people. In the end, however, Aryan genes reassert themselves, the Jew Süss is hanged, and his remains are exhibited publicly in an iron cage.

The film, a great crowd pleaser, made Moshe's "blood boil. I was red in the face when I came out." He was mortified, humiliated, outraged, and shamed. "The way in which jealousy, hatred, and loathing are aroused is simply indescribable." In the film a Jew was made to say: "We, too, have a God, but this God is the Lord of Vengeance." Moshe could not believe it: "This is a lie, pure and simple," he protested. "Our Lord is the same Lord who said: 'Love thy neighbor as thyself,' but now I pray He may appear as a Lord of Vengeance." The film reconfirmed his belief that without some miracle "our end is as sure as I am sitting here. For not only the body of Israel is attacked, but also its spirit."

Moshe's reaction to *Jew Süss* is reminiscent of Yitzhak's response to the "Badge of Shame" and David's to the poster of Jewish shopkeepers adding dirty water, rat meat, and worms to the food. "God grant that this shame may soon end," David had cried. But Moshe went further. He realized that *Jew Süss* was part of that general strategy by which Hitler meant to make good on his promise to spread anti-Semitism until there were no Jews left. "The Jews are being made so hateful to the world that nothing that anyone can do will be able to undo his work. When I left the cinema, I realized the nature of the fiend. . . ."

Though it hurt Moshe no end to see Jews constantly defamed, there was nothing for it but to bite his lip— "Who has a mind for honor in times of such distress?"—as at the graduation ceremony held at the commercial school he was attending. Rising with his fellow students to honor the Belgian national anthem, he felt

as if a knife had pierced my heart, and I inwardly contracted with pain. I suddenly became aware of the unique hardship our homeless people endure. Here before me stood a people in whom the spiritual level of achievement and authority is not of the most advanced, and yet, after the playing of some of their national songs, they rose as one to sing their anthem and pay homage to their nation. At that moment I thought of our nation's dignity and how it is daily being systematically degraded in every conceivable fashion by our enemies.

But never was Moshe more humiliated than the time he was forced to lie about his name. This happened while he was sitting in a café with a schoolmate and some girls and boys he had not met before. Listening to their chatter and laughter and watching them flirt, he became aware that this was "the first time I had ever been in such company," and reflected:

> I asked myself what are the real spiritual values of these boys and girls, who may well be regarded as a typical sample. While such terrible events are going on, while millions of young people are being plucked in the bud, while millions more risk their lives for the sake of ideas, whether correct or distorted but at least with the honest and consecrated intention of ensuring the world a better future—at the same time, these boys and girls sit there and by their expressions you would never guess that anything had happened in the world or that lawlessness and violence are the order of the day. Shallow youth, with neither ideas nor ideals, without any kind of content whatever, really completely worthless.

As he sat there, lost in thought, somebody suddenly asked his name. The problem was that his name identified him "as a member of a certain group who is hated everywhere. Therefore I never give people my right name," Moshe explained. Caught off guard, he swallowed hard and blurted out: "My name is Harry"—and was immediately overcome by shame. "And as I said that, it seemed to me that I had lost merit. Before these terrible times I would never have dreamed of hiding the smallest detail of my origin and give the impression that I was ashamed of it. However, times change." He felt disgraced, Moshe continued, not so much because he had to deny who and what he was, but because these boys and girls "had served as a standard to which I had tried to adjust my own values." Moshe doubted his own worth, too. "What are my cultural and spiritual values that I can cite as a standard or as a barricade against temptation?" he asked. "In fact I am merely an empty vessel, with nothing of worth in me. That is the real truth."

"EVERYTHING NOW SEEMS POINTLESS, WORTHLESS"

Moshe waged a constant battle with the forces that sapped his spirit and emptied his life of meaning. "I am idle all day long," he wrote on November 24, 1942, "and have nothing to do. A few weeks ago I registered in the lending library for Hebrew and Yiddish books. I read a lot—all sorts of Hebrew books—but this does not cheer me up. I feel that I am sinking lower and lower." "These days I don't want to do much," he reported on December 7, 1942. "When you are waiting for miracles and nothing happens, you can't find any drive or willpower within yourself." It was Hanukkah, the Jewish Feast of Lights.

A couple of weeks later, having learned that "a hundred thousand [Jews] had already been killed in the East," Moshe was "indifferent to everyone and everything. Nothing I read arouses my interest." A few months later (February 12, 1943), the same story: "During recent days an emptiness has formed inside me. Nothing motivates me to do anything or write anything, and no new ideas enter my mind; everything is as if asleep. . . . Yes, I think that the holy spark which I always felt within me has been taken from me, and here I am, without spirit, without thought, without anything, and all I have is my miserable body." April 7, 1943: "During recent days I have been gripped by terrible sensations of loneliness, isolation, and dejection."

When Moshe said he was idle, he meant only one thing: that he "did nothing to better my soul or to elevate my spirit." It was the thought of using his time purposefully that gave him the idea of starting a diary, "so that I can write in it every day what I do and think. . . ." Sometimes he missed a day. "Once again about two weeks have passed since I last wrote in my diary," he confessed on September 3, 1943, "but this doesn't bother me as it used to. The contrary is the case, because for some time now my diary has become a reflection of my spiritual life, and when I am not thinking much or my spiritual life seems to stagnate, it would be wrong of me to force myself to write and thus violate the quality of all that I have written previously."

"The terrible events of these days make everything seem tiny, as if viewed through the wrong end of a microscope," he complained; "the greater the troubles, the smaller everything seems. . . . Everything now seems pointless, worthless." This he found to be true even of the Bible, the only book he had brought with him from The Hague. He resolved to read some Bible every day in the hope that "the Lord's promise to Joshua, 'And then you shall become wise,' will be fulfilled in me." Yet he found "nothing in it." Every Sunday he borrowed books and journals from the lending library of the Jewish community center, but he did not get much pleasure from them. He considered many of the subjects and thoughts of the authors worthless. Moshe was annoyed when someone's name was mentioned "about a thousand times" just because he had founded a Hebrew-language magazine for teaching Jews the natural sciences. "I said to myself: 'These people are really children.' " "It struck me that lifetimes can be devoted to studying the most insignificant things," he said of an article on the location of the soul. "I am sure that a clever man could study a piece of wood or a stone for all his life and could fill innumerable books with the results of his investigation." Poetry? Moshe dismissed it out of hand. This was not the time for it.

Yet there was a day even Moshe felt happy, though

he did not say why. "Yes, I am happy," he reported on July 18, 1943. "I cannot and do not want to deny it."

> If you ask me what I am happy about, I would answer that I feel a gladness that only serves to underscore my pain, that emphasizes our troubles, and that deepens and renews our constantly bleeding wounds. Yes, this joy is of the same kind as those pitiful drops of water that only intensify thirst. For how can I escape the troubles of my people? How can I avoid their anguish that is also mine? The joy of this day has made me feel more insistently the agony of my dear people.

Moshe was consumed by guilt. Jews were being deported, "and I sit here in Brussels, seemingly quiet, carefree, and lacking nothing," he wrote in the first month of 1943. "Yes, that is the way it seems, and in fact that is what I think sometimes, but when I lie in bed at night and examine my situation at all closely, then I see just how much I lack. I, too, wish to suffer with my brothers, with my people, whom I love so much. My people, my people!" When he thought about his life in Brussels and the advice of a Jewish teacher in The Hague who had counseled him to flee to Switzerland or unoccupied France in order to save himself "for our people," Moshe did not at all feel that he had been saved; on the contrary, he considered himself "a traitor, who fled from his people at the time of their anguish." Worse: He believed that since he was not suffering enough, he would not be worthy of redemption.

Thoughts of the suffering of his people never left him, "not even for a minute."

> I try so hard to deprive myself of the numerous plea-
> sures that are to be found all around. I walk in the
> street and the sun is burning hot and I am covered
> with perspiration, and then I think of going for a
> swim—immediately afterward I remember where my
> people are and then I cannot even dream of going
> swimming; or I pass a pastry shop and I see in the
> window some attractive, delicious-looking cream cakes
> and I am just about to enter the shop—and then the
> situation of my brothers flashes across my mind and my
> desires are destroyed, and I am overcome with shame
> for having forgotten their plight.

Moshe even considered signing up for "labor" in the east so he could be with his Jewish brothers and sisters. "Often have I felt this yearning and need to be with them and participate in their sufferings. . . . [The Germans] also need workers in Poland and the lands of the east, so that should I go to the Germans and say that I wish to go and work then they would doubtlessly take me. But at least for the time being, I am sure that my father would not let me do any such thing."

FRIENDS

"Moshe, how would you like to go to school to learn typing and shorthand?" his father asked one day. "I re-plied that if my father wished it, I would not refuse. . . ." A week later he was pounding a type-writer. Moshe did not complain, however, except about the students.

> I get there at nine in the morning and sit and pound the typewriter; then some girls who also study there enter and they are full of laughter, joy, and gaiety. And already, this sight—I mean seeing these impudent girls, laughing and gay at a time when the girls of my people are wretched and have not known the happiness these girls enjoy—excited in me jealousy and hatred for them. But that is not all. When they sit down and I hear them tell each other where they were the night before, what movie they saw, who their boyfriends are, or what love letters they have received, then because of my great jealousy as I remember our people, I am on the verge of tears. At such times I don't think so much of the physical affliction of my people as of their spiritual anguish, which may well be greater than their physical pain. I know full well how bitter it is when children have nothing to eat and when their parents can give them nothing—but how much more bitter it is when the entire youth of a nation is sad, when its young girls no longer laugh and its young men are melancholy.

How people could be gay in time of war was beyond him. What's more, Moshe thought that living amid carnage actually drove their pleasure up a notch, as he reflected in January 1943, after learning that a family of four Jews he had known, a husband and wife and their two children, had been rounded up by the Germans.

I see in the streets that the gentiles are happy and gay, and that nothing touches them. It is like being in a great hall where many people are joyful and dancing and also where there are a few people who are not happy and who are not dancing. And from time to time, a few people of this latter kind are taken away, led to another room, and strangled. The happy, dancing people in the hall do not feel this at all. Rather, it seems as if this adds to their joy and doubles their happiness.

In the summer of 1943, Moshe had become friendly with one of his classmates, and through him had met other boys and girls. He could not stop himself from seeing them, "not even for a single day," "despite my feeling the awful shallowness of their lives." But on July 14, he decided to break with them for good, "convinced as I am of their complete lack of even the slightest content or worth. . . ."

It was at times like these that Moshe experienced a great longing for the friends he had been forced to leave behind in The Hague. One Sabbath evening in January 1943, he cried—for only the third time in his life, he confessed. He thought of two people he had met at Hebrew school in The Hague. "The first is the girl I loved and still love." Moshe did not mention her name: They had hardly ever spoken. "Who knows where this girl is now?" he asked. Her image kept floating before his eyes "in all her beauty."

Whenever he thought of her, he inevitably thought of Finkel, his dearest friend in The Hague. They would sit together during lunch and study the Talmud. "He was an amiable, openhearted boy." He, too, was in love with a girl but, unlike Moshe, had not been afraid to let her know. Moshe found this remarkable, in that Finkel was a member of an ultrareligious group and the girl was not at all religious. Every time he thought of Finkel and "the girl," and "all my people . . . the tears appeared as if by themselves and I could not hold them back."

In The Hague, Moshe had never felt a need to pour out his heart to a friend.

> I always would tell myself that it is only a manifestation of a kind of softheartedness that I have always despised. . . . But from then until now, I find myself completely changed. I didn't know then what it was to live without knowing anyone even a little, without having anyone, to be as lonely as if one were in a desert. Oh, how I wish I could see some of my old friends; how my soul longs to talk with my friend Finkel.

The friendships Moshe made in Brussels were superficial. He had to hide that he was a Jew, so he could have no real friends. He tried hard to make friends with a Jewish boy he had known in The Hague, "but the spirit of our conversations was altogether different from what I had imagined it would be, and so I received yet another disappointment." Only Marcel Dutranges, an older schoolmate, made a difference in his life. Marcel was the son of the people he had stayed with when he first came to Brussels. Moshe was impressed with his honesty and good-heartedness. But Marcel left for England in July 1943.

THE   BIBLE   AND   ISRAEL

Every morning Moshe faced southeast, eyes humbly cast down, feet firmly planted next to each other, and recited the Eighteen Benedictions. He changed some of the blessings "to supplications in order to adapt them, insofar as possible, to the terrible magnitude of our troubles." He also added one, imploring "that the Lord should see our degradation. . . ." During Hanukkah 1942, Moshe prayed more fervently than ever before. But afterward he wondered if it served any purpose at all to offer up his prayers for deliverance and salvation with so much sincerity, seeing how little merit he had. But then he thought of his exalted namesake, "our first and best leader, Moses," and he took heart.

> He, too, was all alone and yet rose to greatness. And there are many other similarities between his situation and mine. I often wonder how I can improve myself. I cannot travel anywhere. But then I think of Moses—he traveled extensively and did not try to do good to all men but just to his small circle. Nevertheless, he reached the status of Prophet of Prophets and Prince of Princes. He did not attain his stature easily, as he had to work and enslave his spirit for eighty years, as our teachers have carefully pointed out. Only after eighty years was he worthy.

The greatest of the Jewish prophets also served Moshe as a shining example for self-improvement. "I am irritable by nature and lose my temper easily, but by the example of the man whose name was the same as mine, I must make an effort to overcome this side of my nature," wrote Moshe toward the end of 1942. "But every time I have resolved to do this, I have gotten into an argument with one of my sisters and forgotten all my good resolutions. But now I am writing down in black and white that I will strive not to lose my temper easily or, better still, not to lose my temper at all."

It was not just the example of his celebrated namesake from which Moshe drew strength and comfort; it was all of Jewish history. Past and present became one, interchangeable.

> Every time I read those chapters that speak of the future, of the end of days, of the time of Israel's troubles, I feel from every letter, from every single part of every letter, these words refer to the present. They must refer to these days or else I would not find them so consoling that when I read them peace and quiet come over me.

During Hanukkah 1942, Moshe was struck by the topicality of the words in the last stanza of the popular and powerful hymn, *Maoz Tzur* ("A Strong Fortress"). *Maoz Tzur* pleads for deliverance from the foes that had attempted to destroy the Jews in the past. Moshe copied the last stanza, adding his own exclamation mark:

Reveal Thy sacred mighty arm
And draw redemption near.
Take Thy revenge upon that
Wicked people (!) that has shed the blood
Of those who worship Thee.
Our deliverance has been long overdue,
Evil days are endless,
Banish the foe, destroy the shadow of his image,
Provide us with a guiding light.

Finally, there was Zionism. Zionism was the political movement that strove for the reestablishment of a Jewish homeland in the Middle East. Launched in Europe toward the end of the nineteenth century, Zionism was the Jewish equivalent of the nationalisms that were then sweeping Europe. Whether they were Slavs, Finns, Serbs, Hungarians, or Irish, many Europeans came to believe that any distinct people had to have a nation of their own, a country in which they could speak their own language, practice their own faith— and exclude or rule over all others. This growing nationalism affected Jews in two ways. On the one hand, it meant that an increasing number of people saw them as outsiders and discriminated against them, or wanted to remove them from their new nations altogether. On the other, a considerable number of Jews, especially those in Eastern Europe, where persecution was rampant, felt a renewed yearning for a state of their own. Those who worked for the establishment of a Jewish state were called Zionists.

The expectation that one day Jews might have a

country of their own made Moshe's heart beat faster. In Palestine, Moshe felt, Jews would "live as one nation in one country, with the one and only God." In March 1943, sunk in gloom, he took a Palestine almanac out from the Jewish library, and that changed his state of mind.

> The name of the almanac is "My Homeland." How many times have I not said this word to myself in the last week, and each time it comes into my mind I am filled with yearning for it, and my soul longs for my country that I have loved—and still love—so much. . . . But now this love and yearning have greatly increased. For it is only now that I feel how much we need a country in which we could live in peace as every people lives in its country. Each time I stand to say the Eighteen Benedictions, I direct my whole soul to my lovely land, and I see it before my eyes; I see the coast, I see Tel Aviv, Jaffa, and Haifa. Then I see Jerusalem, with the Mount of Olives, and I see the Jordan as it flows from Lebanon to the Dead Sea. I also see the land across the Jordan—I visualize all this when I stand to pray. . . . Oh, how my soul yearns for you, my homeland, how my eyes crave for the sight of you, my country, the Land of Israel.

Moshe condemned those who had opposed Zionism, holding them morally responsible for "every being" who had not gone to the Promised Land because of them. He believed that with a state of their own, Jews would be able to deal with non-Jews as equals and no longer be merely a "nation of victims"—"dead live

people or the living dead"—but of "soldiers or farm-
ers." On the radio one day, he heard a speech by Nazi
propaganda chief Joseph Goebbels urging sacrifice for
the sake of the nation, and came away impressed. If
only Jews would have some of that spirit, Moshe remarked, but without the "all-encompassing mania, in
the name of which millions of people are sacrificed on
the altar of the fatherland." Then, if they had to fight
and die, as in Palestine, they would at least do so as
"free Jews—and not like those of my brothers who are
now suffering under the atrocious Germans, who lead
them like sheep to be slaughtered."

But there were other reasons as well why Moshe
thought Jews ought to go to Palestine. He foresaw a
possibility that after the war—that is, after an Allied
victory—Jews would remain in Europe and be exposed
to a danger "seven times greater" than what they were
facing now: "final assimilation." From "the national religious Jewish point of view," Moshe insisted, this
should not be the "sequel to our suffering and all the
pains that we have endured and still are enduring." But
he doubted Jews were ready for such a change. Jews
were "so exile-minded that many generations would
have to pass before we become a free people physically
and mentally (the latter is the main thing). That is why
we will need leaders to guide us on the road to true
spiritual freedom."

> Two thousand years / Have we been in exile
> Two thousand years / Have we been suffering
> Two thousand years / Have we been hoping

For our long-delayed salvation.
Two thousand years / Have we been wandering
Two thousand years / Have we been moving
Two thousand years / Have we been yearning
For our long-delayed redemption.
And now we / Are standing here.
In this year of the / Twentieth Century
We stand here / and yearn
O Lord, shalt Thou help?
Yes, Our Lord / Thou shalt help
Yes, our Redeemer / Thou shalt redeem
Thou hast forgotten / And shalt remember
Thou hast neglected / And shalt return
Thou shalt return / And restore us
Thou shalt have pity / And have mercy on us
Thou shalt plant us / In our land
And shalt rebuild us / In our country.

"MY FUTURE"

Moshe realized that the world had reached an important juncture. He read the newspapers and drew his conclusions. In August 1943 the war was going well for the Allies. The Americans and the British had invaded Sicily, and on the other side of Europe the Russians were driving the Germans west. Connecting the Anglo-American invasion of Sicily and the Russian attack, Moshe concluded: "It must mean that they [the British and Americans] also wish to drive into the heart of Europe and not allow the Russians to take it all for themselves."

A few weeks later, the Anglo-American forces having invaded mainland Italy, Moshe took this view a step further. The English and Americans, he asserted, had recognized the Russian desire to smash right through to central Europe and were doing their best to forestall it by intensifying their attacks on Germany.

> I now see that Germany is fighting for its very existence as a sovereign nation, for it is very possible that after the war Germany will continue to exist, but only as a tool in the hands of its conquerors. It may be said that Germany has up to now, in great measure, been an instrument in the hands of the English and Americans, who have hoped that the Germans would drain the strength of the Russians. It looks as though the English and Americans have seriously underestimated Russia's power and now fear her very much. One may deduce this from the many, frequent, and long conferences that take place between the heads of state and chiefs of staffs of England and America. Recently these conferences have become much more numerous, and even now, as I write, Churchill is meeting with Roosevelt [in Quebec].
>
> In this way one may see clear the evidence of a coming war between England and America on one side and Russia on the other.

It is not surprising that Moshe paid a great deal of attention to what was going on in the world. He had decided to become a diplomat in the state of Israel, "a leader of his people," "a Jewish statesman in the Land of Israel." "Only there shall I be able to achieve my object of helping my people, which is my only wish and lifelong aspiration." He did not think becoming a diplomat would require "a great deal of study." The most important qualities were the ability "to use one's head," "a strong character and a heart of steel—those, and the help of the Lord."

It was to this end that he began studying Arabic, on his own and without a teacher, with a German book as his text. Throughout the diary, he mentioned his progress and his problems, not the least of which was the lack of someone to help him with pronunciation. Yet he persevered, not because he liked it "or anything like that," but because he realized that Palestine was no empty land, and "a large part of the inhabitants of the land of Israel and the surrounding countries speak it." To Moshe it was "obvious that we shall have to live in peace with our brothers, the sons of Ishmael, who are also Abraham's descendants." He was convinced that the riots in British Palestine in the thirties had been "incited by Germany and Italy" and could have been prevented had Jewish leaders been able to speak Arabic. "And therefore I am trying very hard to learn the language."

In a section headed "My Future," dated May 19, 1943, he devoted a long passage to analyzing his conflicted feelings about this future:

> When I first got this idea and wrote it in my diary, I tried to do all I could to bring it about. . . . But after some time had passed I saw, and what is more important I felt, that it was all worthless. . . . I studied a lot

of Arabic. But as the war grew more and more terrible, I came to feel that if results of lasting value were to come out of it, that is, if we attain the redemption for which our people has been waiting and hoping for two thousand years, then these cannot occur through diplomacy or other deceit or by the grace of the great powers. In that case, there is no longer any value to the Arabic I am studying and my activities in this direction would appear to be useless. Thus, nearly all the positive content to my life is shown to be pointless, and I am left with almost nothing. My great complaint is against this terrible emptiness. I now understand that ideas and thoughts are worthless if one cannot convert them into action.

But two and a half months later, snapping back, he again wrote confidently of starting a "new life, dedicated to my people."

It was not to be. The final, undated, diary entry is headed, "Twilight, the hour of the Minha [afternoon] prayer."

I am sitting at the window and readying myself for the Minha prayer. I look out, and I see that all is red, the whole horizon is red. The sky is covered with bloody clouds, and I am frightened when I see it. I say to myself: "Where do these clouds come from, bleeding clouds, where are you from?" . . . Don't you know? They come from the seas of blood. These seas have been brought about by millions of Jews who have been captured and who knows where they are. . . . We are the bleeding clouds, and from the seas of blood have

we come. We have come to you from the place where
your brothers are, to bring you greetings from your
people. We are witnesses; we were sent by our people
to show you their trouble; we were brought into being
by an inferno of suffering; and we are a sign of peace
to you. . . .

Two thousand years have we brought into this world
children who are doomed to suffer. Lord our God, is
this still not enough? . . . Wilt Thou forget us forever,
Lord of Israel? . . . Pity us, have mercy, Lord, on Thy
people, do not tarry, do not wait, for soon it will be
too late. . . .

Moshe was right: It *was* late. Salvation did not come.
Betrayed, the Flinkers were arrested on April 7, 1944,
Passover Eve, the holiday that celebrates the Jews' deliverance from Egyptian slavery. The Flinkers were sent
to Auschwitz, where Moshe and his parents were murdered. His younger brother and his five sisters survived.
Upon their return from the camp, the Flinker sisters
found the diary in the basement of the Brussels apartment building where they had lived during the war.

Mariska started packing, and Grandma went on ironing the men's shirts on the porch as though she hadn't heard a word of what was said. Mariska read in the notice that we are allowed to take along only one change of underwear, the clothes on our bodies and the shoes on our feet, but Grandma just went on ironing and ironing. And all the while she even hummed to herself, and I had never heard her sing before. . . . All the while I thought I was just having a bad dream, that I would wake up and the dream would disappear. . . . I know it isn't a dream, but I can't believe a thing. . . . I am busy all day making coffee for Uncle Béla, but Grandma drinks cognac. Nobody says a word. Dear diary, I have never been so afraid.

CHAPTER 4

Éva Heyman

"I Want to Live!"

"I was born on Friday the thirteenth," Éva Heyman started off the diary she began keeping on her thirteenth birthday, February 13, 1944. That day there was "quite a good party" at which they had "tea with sandwiches and Sacher torte." Past birthdays had been celebrated with hot chocolate with whipped cream, but because of the war there wasn't enough milk. "Besides, drinking tea is more grown-up." From her mother Éva got a gold bracelet, and from her father a pair of high-heeled black shoes and two pairs of sheer stockings, both firsts. Other presents included "a light tan spring coat and a navy-blue knit dress," fourteen books, records, candy, oranges, chocolate, and "a pretty little gold chain," on which, she confided to her diary, she would carry "the key with which I will lock you so that no one will know my secrets." The only sour note that day was that her mother, whom Éva called Ági (from Ágnes), was not around to help celebrate.

She was in Budapest about to have minor surgery. Still, Éva felt her mother could "have managed to come."

"HOW ÁGI'S HEART IS ARRANGED"

Éva grew up in Nagyvárad, Várad for short. Nagyvárad is one those central European towns with a history of being pushed around like a disk on a shuffleboard. One day it was part of Romania; the next, part of Hungary. When Éva was born, it was Romanian and called Oradea. Thirteen years later, when she was murdered, it was Hungarian. Today it is again Romanian and again called Oradea.

In 1940, one in five Nagyvárad residents was Jewish. Most of these 20,000 Jews identified with Hungary in culture and speech. A good example was Éva's maternal grandfather, Dr. Reszsö Rácz, a prosperous pharmacist. Like many Jews in Várad, Dr. Rácz had supported the Hungarian cause when the city had been Romanian, clamoring for national minority rights for Hungarians and hoping the region would become Hungarian again. In 1940 Dr. Rácz got his wish.

Éva well remembered the coming of the Hungarians. Grandfather Rácz's pharmacy was on a corner of Várad's main street. On a beautiful sunny day not long after the takeover, Regent Miklós Horthy rode past it "on a white horse" and waved to the jubilant crowd that lined the sidewalks. Éva watched the procession from the pharmacy window and waved back, which made her mother mad. "She said that when she was still a little girl, Horthy used to murder Jews at Lake Balaton."

Éva also remembered her grandfather's pharmacy being taken away from him. Hungary, following the lead of its German ally, had a number of anti-Jewish laws on the books. One day Dr. Rácz had been summoned to city hall and told to get out because he was "an unreliable Romanian-lover and a Jew." His business was returned to him two months later, thanks largely to the untiring efforts of his daughter Ágnes, Éva's mother. The new owner "left the pharmacy raving mad," recalled Éva, threatening that "Grandpa wouldn't die in bed, but in quite a different way altogether."

At the time, Éva's mother was still living in Nagyvárad. Later, she moved to Budapest with her second husband, Béla Zsolt, leaving Éva with her grandparents in Nagyvárad, about 150 miles away. Until 1944 Ági visited regularly, and immediately prior to and after the German invasion of Hungary in mid-March, she spent all her time with her daughter.

Éva's family was well off. Her father, Béla Heyman, was an architect from a rich and prominent family. The Heymans owned a hotel "full of Persian rugs and beds," Éva wrote, "a movie theater, shops, and apartments." Éva's stepfather—Uncle Béla, in the diary—was a well-known Hungarian writer and journalist. Éva's mother was a pharmacist, as well. The grandparents, with whom Éva lived, employed a cook, Mariska, and a governess named Juszti, who had also been Éva's mother's governess.

Éva's mother and stepfather were socialists. When

Hitler invaded Poland, Ági and Béla were living in Paris. Afraid she would not see her daughter for many years if she remained in France, she kept pestering her husband "till Uncle Béla couldn't stand to see her suffer anymore, and they came back to Budapest." As a Jew, journalist, and socialist, Béla Zsolt (born Steiner) was a marked man. A law passed in 1939 restricting the participation of Jews in public and economic life had made it impossible for him to continue writing under his own name, and in the spring of 1944 his works were banned altogether. Éva admired her "uncle" immensely, because "he knows a lot, more than anyone else I know." Ágnes shared her husband's politics, but she also "likes pretty dresses," gossiped her daughter. "She talks only about politics and books when she is with her friends. But with Grandma or when she's alone with a friend, the conversation also turns to dresses, in whispers, in the next room."

Éva was crazy about her mother. Ági was beautiful—"more beautiful than Greta Garbo," gushed her father—intelligent, and utterly devoted to her second husband. "Grandma says that there isn't another soul Ági loves besides Uncle Béla, not even me," wrote Éva on her thirteenth birthday. "But I don't believe it. It may be that when I was little she didn't love me, but she loves me now." Later, she speculated:

> I think that Ági loves Uncle Béla more than anyone else in the world. Then me, and then Grandpa. Of course, she never gives an honest answer when I ask

her. She says: The love a woman has for the fruit of
her womb is different from the love she has for her
husband, her parents, and her friends. I don't understand how Ági's heart is arranged, but still have the impression that even in her heart she has a scale of
priorities, although she denies it.

Éva was jealous of her mother, even though she
thought jealousy "an ugly trait." Ági knew it too and
instructed her mother that whenever she gave her anything, she should buy something for her granddaughter
as well. Ági also told her mother "that it's better not to
pay any attention to the fact that I'm jealous," reported
Éva. "Every child has its faults. Ági has known children
who always lied, and even stole. And I really hardly
ever tell lies, mostly in school, or to my French
teacher, when I haven't done my homework, and I say
that I had a headache or a toothache. But I couldn't
possibly steal, no matter what!"

As for her daughter, Ági assured her she'd get over it
when she grew up, and urged her to go with her to
visit the poor Jewish children on the other side of
town, because it wasn't good for her "always to see
only the children I go to the Lyceum [academic high
school] with."

And I will realize how they live there in poverty, without enough to eat, with torn shoes, no heat in winter
because they have no money for firewood. If only I
thought of orphans and sick children, I would be
cured of my jealousy. Then I would be grateful for

having everything I need and not having any responsibilities except the responsibility to study.

Curiously Ági, otherwise so shrewd, did not seem to
notice that the problem was lack of attention; specifi-
cally, her own absence. But Éva knew. Visiting her
friend Anikó on the afternoon of February 17, 1944,
three days after she began keeping her diary, Éva noticed that "every so often" Anni kept jumping up to
kiss her parents. "In order to give Ági a kiss," Éva
complained, "I usually have to travel quite a long way,
and in order to kiss my father I have to walk two
blocks on the main street without being sure that I'll
even find him at home."

Juszti, Éva's governess, knew it too. Juszti had been
with the Rácz household for thirty years, and Éva admired her "more than anyone else in the world, maybe
even more than Ági." Neither she nor the rest of the
family thought of Juszti as a servant; "she was the best
of us all," wrote Éva, quoting her mother, "and it's
true." When Juszti, who was Austrian, was no longer
allowed to live with them, Éva cried her eyes out and
didn't go to school for two days. Her grandfather had
tried to get around the ban by paying a local waiter to
marry her so that she could become a Hungarian cit-
izen; "but he wanted the thousand pengös in advance,
even before marrying Juszti," Éva recalled, "so the
whole thing was called off."

Juszti, who had never married and had no children,
loved Éva as her own flesh and blood. After the war,
she wrote a letter to Ági in which she explained what
had really gone on inside Éva.

Éva loved you very much. . . . You were her ideal, because she considered you beautiful and wise. . . . She
never said so, but I always felt that she never forgave
you for getting divorced and going to Budapest without her. . . .

She also loved your husband, loved him very much,
even though she naturally saw him as the obstacle to
your living together. . . . If she bore any grudge, it was
under no circumstances directed against Béla, but only
against you.

Éva was happiest when with her mother. In Nagyvárad
they went swimming in the pool by the river and visited the Bishop's Palace, Éva's favorite place. The palace, today a museum of archaeology, ethnography, and
history, has 365 windows, one for each day of the year.
When her mother visited the palace as a child, Éva re-
vealed, she had darted around wanting to look out of
every one of them. In Budapest's City Park, that lush
oasis in the center of the city, they rode the roller
coaster, and Ági "almost fainted from the loop-the-
loop, and she turned completely white, but in the zoo
she had as much fun as I did." And when Juszti came
along and the three of them wandered around Pest
(Budapest is divided by the Danube River into two
halves, Buda and Pest), Éva's happiness was complete.
"In Pest we always had fun pretending that Ági was my
big sister and Juszti our governess. In those days Ági
was still very gay. . . ."

"ARYANS WILL ALWAYS BE BETTER OFF"

Éva couldn't wait for the war to be over. Then she would become a "Budapest girl" and live with her mother and Uncle Béla—"we'll have an apartment of our own and we'll also have money, because there won't be any Jewish Law for journalists."

When the war was over, she would marry an "Aryan Englishman" and become a photographer—because then her mother would love her more, for Ági loved the English, and because "Aryans will always be better off." She envied Klódi, "the prettiest girl in the class," like her the daughter of divorced parents. Klódi's father was Jewish and lived in Nagyvárad. But her mother was "not only French but even Aryan. So Klódi is a mixture, one half Jewish like her father and the other half Aryan like her mother." After the eighth grade, Éva recounted, Klódi was "going to live with her French grandmother, and there she'll be an Aryan." But not to worry: "Grandpa says that by the time I get married it won't matter whether my husband is Jewish or not. My grandfather even thinks that by that time people won't even know what the word 'Aryan' meant."

But now it did seem to matter. Both sides of Éva's family were assimilated Jews. None of them appears to have observed any of the Jewish holidays. Ági's parents had changed their name from Rosenberg to Rácz. The "tragedy of us Jews," Uncle Béla explained to Éva, was that if the richest man in Várad happened to be a Jew, "then the Aryans hate me, too, because I am also Jewish, even though I really don't have any money stashed away."

Béla Zsolt and his wife were fighting for a world in which all racial and religious distinctions would disappear. Ági told her daughter that she "should always be for the Left, because then everybody has a good life and the wicked people are killed." Consequently, Éva confided to her diary that after she became a photographer, she wouldn't "photograph a single Rightist because I hate them with all my might!"

One day Éva was visiting the estate of the Poroszlays, the people for whom Juszti had started working after she had been forced out of her job with the Ráczes, when two other guests "started cursing the Jews right in front of me. Once I even happened to overhear Poroszlay say to Aunt Boriska, his wife, that right now I was still a very pretty girl, but when I grew up my racial character would show."

"Uncle" Poroszlay—it was common for Hungarian children to address even strangers as Aunt or Uncle—was right about one thing: Éva was a very pretty girl. Blonde, braids, perfect teeth, charming smile. And she knew it, too, since everybody kept reminding her of it. "Grandma says that I'll be even prettier than Ági, and that she's only charming but I'll have a modern figure. That's because I do a lot of athletics, swimming, skating, bicycle riding, and exercise."

There must have been a lot of talk in the Rácz-Heyman clan about "Aryan" versus "Jewish" looks. Éva did not expect to lose her blessed Aryan looks. It was in the genes: Her father did not at all look like a Jew, Éva exulted. "He is so tall and straight, and he has blue eyes like those masculine Aryan types in *Signal* [a Nazi magazine similar to *Life*]. . . . My father really looks like an Aryan and is a very handsome man." Indeed, Béla Heyman had taken the final, seemingly logical, step and converted to Catholicism.

Pista Vadas was a Jew, and a swarthy one at that, but Éva fell "in love" with him. She told her mother how she felt about Pista, thinking that she "would be very cross, because Pista Vadas isn't an Englishman or an Aryan." But Ági took the news good-naturedly, calling him "a handsome bronze bull." Still, Éva was offended, "because now I always think of it whenever I think about Pista." She was relieved, however, that her mother didn't tell her, as her grandmother used to, "that it is very shameless of me to run after boys, and that the only thing I have on my mind is boys."

Being a Jew was regarded as a great burden, the source of endless troubles. Even the assimilated Uncle Béla was sent to the Ukraine. Her stepfather was among the tens of thousands of Jews attached to Hungary's Second Army as laborers, maintaining roads, repairing bridges, removing mines. The Second Army fought the Russians in the east, where Béla spent fifteen months. He did not talk about his experiences in the Ukraine, at least not in front of Éva, but she must have heard the stories that were going around: Jews having to walk hundreds of miles in ice and snow and being hosed down in the middle of winter to become "ice statues." Hungarian Jews were among the first to report the massacres being perpetrated by special killer commandos operating in the east behind the advancing German Army. Béla was one of the few Jews to return from the Ukraine, which was all the more remarkable considering he was in his early forties. "I don't think I'll ever forget that day they carried Uncle Béla off to the Ukraine," wrote Éva. She remembered it so well because from that moment her mother changed completely. It was the summer of 1942, and Béla and Ági were vacationing in Várad:

> We heard the choppy ringing of the long-distance telephone exchange. It was Budapest calling to say that the conscription order had come. Ági said: "This is the end." From that moment she didn't eat a bite and didn't say a word, even though she was usually a big talker. She cried in the street when she went to buy Uncle Béla a knapsack, military shoes, and all sorts of hiking equipment. I thought that one day all those things would be mine, because Uncle Béla was older than the others who were taken and they would certainly let him come back. . . . Uncle Béla was also in the last war, but then he was a soldier, because only in this war Jews go to the front unarmed.

From then on Ági tearfully followed every military development on the Russian front. But Éva's mother did not stay in Várad and cry. From the moment Béla left, Ági fought to get her husband back. She went back to Budapest, saying: "If there is anything at all that I can do for him, that will be possible only in Budapest, and it is my duty to try." Few gave her a chance. Only her mother, Éva's grandmother, was convinced her daughter would pull it off—"because where Uncle Béla is concerned," she told Éva, "not even Hitler himself can stop Ági."

Fifteen months later, Béla was back in Budapest—and jailed. So Ági spent another four months working to get him released. "Grandpa used to say," recalled Éva, "Ági is walking inside the lion's cage . . . and Grandma was constantly in terror that Ági might be arrested because she even went to places where it was written: 'Jews not admitted.' "

When the war was over, Éva predicted, "nobody will go to the Ukraine anymore . . . because it won't matter anymore whether one is a Jew or not." When the war was over, "Uncle Béla might even be a minister," Éva exclaimed, "and then we'll have a really fine apartment in Pest, and we'll even have a car." And when the war was over, she hoped to finally have a Zeiss-Ikon camera.

MÁRTA'S STORY

One of Éva's good friends was Márta Münzer. Márta's father managed a bookstore and advertising agency in Várad. In 1941, all Jews with foreign nationality were ordered to register with the authorities, and Mr. Münzer, being one of those, complied. The so-called alien Jews, of which there were some thirty to thirty-five thousand, were told that they would be sent to

Poland, where they would live in the homes of Jews who had fled east. They did go to Poland, to a place called Kamenets-Podolsk. But there were no homes waiting—only machine guns—and some twenty-three thousand were shot: the first five-figure massacre in the Nazi's Final Solution program. The second entry of the diary, February 14, 1944, told Márta's story:

Márta was two years older than I. Ági said that she was a genius in dance and resembled Josephine Baker. . . . I was always very proud that a genius two classes ahead of me was my friend. That afternoon, it will be three years this summer, Márta was over at our house. First we went riding our bicycles. . . . That was my first "tour" on this bicycle. Márta's was just like mine, only hers was a brighter red. Then we came home, and Ági asked Márta to dance something to music from a record, but Márta didn't want to because she was tired from riding the bicycle. Then we had an afternoon snack, chocolate with whipped cream and strawberries with whipped cream, which Márta loved more than anything else, even more than dancing. Suddenly the bell at the front gate rang five times. It was Márta's nursemaid, who had stayed on as a cook because Márta didn't need a nursemaid anymore. She came in and said: "Mártika, come home. The police are there, and you have to go with Papa and Mama." I still remember Ági. She turned white as the plaster on the walls. But Márta said it must be because she rode her bicycle so fast on Rimanóczi Street, and her father had said many times that she would end up at the police on account of "speeding." That explanation reassured me, but Ági paced up and down the room in such a strange manner, and she kept calling Aunt Pásztor, Márta's grandmother, on the telephone, but there was no answer. In the morning I also called, but there was no answer from Márta's telephone. . . .

The tension then was awful. Ági cried and cried and kept telephoning. . . . Then Ági rushed into town to the journalists, and they told her that tens of thousands of people like Márta and her family had been taken away to Poland in a train, without luggage and without food. They said that if Aunt Münzer hurried up and got a divorce, she and Márta might be allowed to stay. But they didn't want to get divorced. And Márta didn't want to stay here without her father. . . . Márta's bicycle was left near mine, beside the gate, and we didn't have the heart to send it to Márta's grandmother. Ági cried a lot whenever she saw the two red bicycles standing alongside each other. . . .

A month after writing down "Márta's story," Éva had far happier tidings: "The Ágis are here." She was overjoyed, and in a burst of generosity wiped the slate clean. She forgave her mother for not spending the previous Christmas with her (she was in Budapest trying to get her husband out of military prison). Forgiven, too, was her absence at her thirteenth birthday party. But now they were all together. "Dear diary, it's so different with the Ágis at home that I don't care if the war goes on for a long time! But that's disgusting of me, because so many people are suffering. What I mean is that the most wonderful thing in the world is when the whole family is always together. For us, that's a very rare thing!"

Ági was happy, too. Her husband was back from the Ukraine and out of prison. "She says that nothing bad can happen now, because Uncle Béla is home."

Their happiness proved to be short-lived. Five days after her mother's arrival, Éva wrote: "Dear diary, you're the luckiest one in the world, because you cannot feel, you cannot know what a terrible thing has happened to us. The Germans have come!" Hungary was the last country in Nazi-occupied Europe with nearly all of its Jewish population, about 850,000, still intact. Despite the anti-Jewish legislation, the punitive labor battalions, and the massacres in 1941, which had claimed Éva's friend Márta, propaganda chief Joseph Goebbels felt that the "Jewish question [was] being solved least satisfactorily by the Hungarians."

"HITLER'S DOGS ARE HERE"

Now "Hitler's dogs are here," wrote Éva on March 19. The impact was immediate. In the last days of March, Jewish leaders from across Hungary were summoned to the capital and informed that anti-Jewish decrees would soon be forthcoming. On the afternoon of March 30, Éva spotted their neighbors being thrown out of their home. "Carrying a little handbag and a basket, they went out through the gate, and outside three German officers were standing. One of them kicked Uncle Waldmann in the behind as he came out through the gateway of his house in order to hand that pretty little house over to the damned Germans." The day after, Jews learned that as of April 5 they would

have to start wearing a yellow star four inches in di-
ameter, "which must be sewn on every outer gar-
ment, jacket or coat." On the appointed day, Mariska,
the former cook, came over and "sewed a star patch
on my spring coat, very firmly, right over my heart."
Later in the day, Éva went out and "met some yellow-
starred people. They were so gloomy, walking with
their heads lowered. Mariska held my hand as though
I were a baby, and we walked quickly." That afternoon, visiting with her grandmother on her father's
side, Éva learned that her great-uncle's hotel was
smashed to pieces, "and the Germans and Hungarians
had stolen everything they could carry." The movie
theater that belonged to her paternal grandmother
also wound up on the German list of items to
be "requisitioned." Telephones were cut off, Jews
were kicked out of their stores. The Jewish hospital
fell to the SS. And the Jewish patients? "Throw
them into the ditch," advised the SS physician in
charge.

Soon it was Éva's turn. April 7:

Today they came for my bicycle. I almost caused a big
drama. You know, dear diary, I was awfully afraid just
by the fact that the policemen came into the house. I
know that policemen bring only trouble with them,
wherever they go. My bicycle had a proper license
plate, and Grandpa had paid the tax for it. That's how
the policemen found it, because it was registered at
City Hall that I have a bicycle. Now that it's all over,
I'm so ashamed about how I behaved in front of the

policemen. So, dear diary, I threw myself on the
ground, held on to the back wheel of my bicycle, and
shouted all sorts of things at the policemen: "Shame
on you for taking away a bicycle from a little girl!
That's robbery." We had saved up a year and a half to
buy the bicycle. . . . I went to the store and took the
bicycle home, only I didn't ride it but led it along with
my hands, the way you handle a big, beautiful dog.
From the outside I admired the bicycle, and even gave
it a name: Friday. I took the name from *Robinson Cru-
soe,* but it suits the bicycle. First of all, because I
brought it home on a Friday, and also because Friday
is the symbol of loyalty, because he was so loyal to
Robinson. . . . One of the policemen was very annoyed and said: "All we need is for a Jewgirl to put on
such a comedy when her bicycle is taken away. No
Jewkid is entitled to keep a bicycle anymore. The Jews
aren't entitled to bread, either; they shouldn't guzzle
everything, but leave food for the soldiers." You can
imagine, dear diary, how I felt when they were saying
this to my face. I had only heard that sort of thing
on the radio, or read it in a German newspaper. Still,
it's different when you read something and when
it's thrown in your face. Especially if it's when they're
taking my bicycle away.

Later the police would be back for the Ráczes' appli-
ances, the linen, "the silverware, the rugs, the paint-
ings, the Venetian mirror," Éva's camera.

Two days after the police "appropriated" Éva's
bicycle, they came for her father—on account of his
family's money, they said. Every day, Éva brought him

lunch at the elementary school where he was being held. Someone there told her that her father had become a hostage, a "security." Éva was puzzled: "Only I don't understand how a human being can be a security."

> At last they let me go in to my father. Most of these securities sat in the yard on the ground. The sick ones lay in the classroom on the bare floor. Papa said it wasn't so terrible, but it was so boring and uncomfortable. . . . When I left him, it occurred to me that when I was going to elementary school, we children always used to be inside the gate and the parents would wait outside the fence to take us home after school. Now adults, even old people, are inside the school fence, and we children are outside. There is no getting away from it: The world is topsy-turvy.

Éva's father was released on April 20. "Interesting, dear diary, but Papa isn't even glad that he has been released. He said that in his opinion, this isn't the end of it, but only the beginning. What else can happen that can be worse than what has happened already? I know: It can only be Poland."

"I LOOKED ON HELPLESSLY"

The Rácz-Zsoltes were a high-strung lot, which was yet another reason Éva was looking forward to marrying her Aryan Englishman—"because the English

aren't so nervous and they're very aristocratic." The arrival of the Germans and the renewed aggressiveness of
their Hungarian collaborators strained the family's
nerves to the utmost: Uncle Béla chain-smoking,
cooped up inside because he was being stalked, his
books and correspondence burning in the stove; Ági
pacing the floor, getting skinnier, mumbling that this
was the end of everything; the grandfather on edge because he could not go to the pharmacy anymore, and
looking "at Ági in such an odd, sad way, and . . .
caressing her all the time, as though he is saying good-
bye to her."

First the grandmother went mad. Ági's mother either screeched and rolled her eyes or stared vacantly in
front of her. When her shrieks rent the air, Éva stuffed
her ears, but "mostly I cry, because I'm afraid of
Grandma Rácz, and still I feel sorry for her." To keep
the old woman quiet, they gave her sedatives and injec-
tions. Éva was not the only one to be scared of her,
and they all gave in to her, mad or not, in the interest
of keeping the peace.

On April 18, a Christian relative, Sanyi Kaufmann,
brought Ági and Béla forged documents and offered to
smuggle them to Budapest that very evening. When
the grandmother heard what was going on, "she threw
herself on the floor and literally screeched. She said
that Ági is a murderer, because if Ági and Uncle Béla
run away they will kill her in their place. She screamed
other terrible things, until Ági gave her word of honor
that nobody would run away, no matter what!"

Shortly thereafter, a Mrs. Jakobi, a gentile dressmaker,

sneaked into the house and offered to take Éva home with her. Again the grandmother started howling that "she was an evil woman and she would sell me to men and then I would also be an evil woman." How could that be? Éva wondered. "Nobody is buying Jewish girls these days."

Earlier, Éva's governess Juszti had sounded out her new Aryan employers about taking Éva in. But old Jew-hating "Uncle" Poroszlay "said that it was out of the question."

There was a suggestion, too, that Éva become Catholic like her father. "It doesn't matter to Ági," remarked Éva. "She is for anything that might help me, but unfortunately there is a Race Law, and it doesn't matter what a person's religion is. . . ."

In short, dear diary, I'm not becoming a Christian, even though Uncle Béla has heard that many people want to. But the Christian priests in Várad still insist that a person can become a Christian only after studying for six months. Uncle Béla also said that the church had failed shamefully! I always thought that priests are holy people and help anybody who is in trouble. But it seems that they help Aryans only. They don't help Jews. Who helps us?

It was not until the war was over that it became clear that the greatest tragedy of all was the tragedy of missed opportunities. The person most aware of it was Éva's governess, Juszti, who blamed both herself and Ági for the fate that befell Éva. "You know," she wrote later to Ági, "the problem wasn't lack of money, but my lack of imagination." Calling herself a petty bourgeois, "an old ass, an early-morning churchgoer," Juszti went on:

Don't think that I don't go out of my mind during the long nights from not having shot that Poroszlay when he wouldn't allow me to hide Éva there. What could I have done? Now, now, when it is too late, now I know that I could have done a great deal! Right up to the last minute I stuck to that idiotic bourgeois notion that all I am is an obedient hired employee, instead of abandoning everything and going off with Éva someplace where we would not have been recognized, and buying her forged papers with the money I had saved. You know, the problem wasn't money, but my lack of imagination. . . . I thought that decency forbade entering into a fictitious marriage with a waiter whom your father bought. . . . I loved Éva more than anything else in the world. You see, that is why I am accusing myself! Who knows how to feel and love as I do; yet when it came to doing something, I was impotent. I looked on helplessly, just like everybody else, at what was happening to you and Éva. I did not do a thing to prevent it, neither with my brain nor by force. All this became clear too late, of course, late beyond repair. . . .

"I HAVE NEVER BEEN SO AFRAID"

Hungarian and German officials charged with carrying out the "Final Solution" in Hungary met on April 4 in the capital and received their instructions. Drawn up by Secretary of State László Endre, the confidential document stated that "Jews would be taken to prearranged assembly centers regardless of age and sex," and that those "earmarked for deportation may take with them no more than the clothes they are actually wearing, two changes of underclothing, food sufficient for 14 days, and 110 pounds of luggage containing bedding, blankets, palliasses, etc. They will not be in possession of cash, jewelry, and other valuables." It took the executioner less than two months to make a clean sweep of the Hungarian countryside, netting 450,000 Jews, one being Éva.

During the final week of April, a small group of Hungarian and German "Jewish experts" spent a few days in Nagyvárad checking out the site for "Jewish Accommodation." The group included roly-poly Dieter Wisliceny, a seasoned veteran in the war against the Jews, and his master, "evacuation" chief Adolf Eichmann. Also on hand was Secretary of State László Endre. A few days later, on May 1, a "very violent gentleman" arrived in Nagyvárad to supervise the concentration of the Jews into two ghettos, one near the center, the other on the outskirts. His name was Theodor Dannecker, local Gestapo chief and member of Eichmann's "Jew Commandos." That same day came the following announcement:

> Jews who are obliged to wear the yellow star are forbidden to leave their homes after the publication of this announcement. For the time being and until the

issuance of other instructions, Jews will be permitted to leave their homes only between 9:00 and 10:00 A.M. With the exception of this period, all of them must stay at home. At the order of the Royal Hungarian Government, I am placing into a ghetto all the Jews compelled to wear the yellow star in Nagyvárad. I call upon all non-Jews holding Jewish valuables to report them to the mayor's office within three days from the publication of this announcement. I shall be in charge of the receipt of such reported valuables. I warn the non-Jewish inhabitants of the municipality that all persons holding Jewish property who fail to declare it within the period cited above will be prosecuted with the greatest severity and immediate measures will be taken for their internment in camps.

It was Mariska, the Ráczes' former cook, who burst in with the news that there would be a ghetto. Éva:

> Mariska started packing, and Grandma went on ironing the men's shirts on the porch as though she hadn't heard a word of what was said. Mariska read in the notice that we are allowed to take along only one change of underwear, the clothes on our bodies, and the shoes on our feet, but Grandma just went on ironing and ironing. And all the while she even hummed to herself, and I had never heard her sing before. . . . All the while I thought I was just having a bad dream, that I would wake up, and the dream would disappear. . . . I know it isn't a dream, but I can't believe a thing. . . . I am busy all day making coffee for Uncle Béla, but

Grandma drinks cognac. Nobody says a word. Dear diary, I have never been so afraid.

Éva and her family packed and then sat around waiting for the police to come get them. Waiting was nerve-racking, the silence, worse. "It wasn't silent the way it usually is at night," noted Éva, "but of a kind that I couldn't even imagine till now." Even her bird, Mandi, wasn't singing. "From time to time, when the bell rang," Éva went on, "I would almost be happy. I knew that we were being taken to the ghetto, but felt that if this silence would go on much longer, we would all go crazy."

Finally, after three days, the doorbell did ring and two policemen showed up to take them to the ghetto. "Then everything happened like in a film." The policemen were "not unfriendly," but one of them insisted that Éva give up the little gold chain around her neck, the one holding the key to the diary.

"Don't you know yet," the policeman said, "that you aren't allowed to keep anything made of gold? This isn't private Jewish property anymore but national property!" . . . Whenever something was being taken from us, Ági would always pretend not to notice at all, because she had an obsession about not letting the policemen think that it bothered us that our things were being taken, but this time she begged the policeman to let me keep the little gold chain. She started sobbing and saying: "Mr. Inspector, please go and ask your colleagues, and they will tell you that I have never begged for anything, but please let the child keep just this little gold chain. You see, she keeps the key to her diary on it." "Please," the policeman said, "that is impossible; in the ghetto you will be checked again. I, so help me God, don't need this chain or any other object that is being taken from you. I don't need any of it, but I don't want any difficulties. I am a married man. My wife is going to have a baby." I gave him the chain. In Grandma's night table I found a velvet ribbon. I asked the policeman: "Mr. Inspector, may I take a velvet ribbon along to the ghetto?" He said I could. Now your key hangs on that velvet ribbon, dear diary.

As they were leaving, Éva noticed that the "garden [had] never looked so beautiful," and that Grandpa stood there looking at it, "shaking from crying. There were also tears in Uncle Béla's eyes. And only now I noticed how Grandma had turned into such an old woman . . . and Grandma Rácz is only fifty-four. She walked out of the gate as though she was drunk or sleepwalking. She didn't even look back, and there wasn't a tear in her eyes. Ági put her hands under the bundle on Grandpa's back so it shouldn't be so heavy for him."

An open truck stood by the gate.

It was impossible to sit, so we stood. They drove us standing up to Várad's main street. When we got to the pharmacy, Grandpa and Ági looked the other way. All the way Uncle Béla held Ági in his arms. I cuddled up alongside Grandma so as not to see the Aryans in the street. They were taking their afternoon strolls, as though it were the most natural thing in the world that from now on we should live in the ghetto. . . .

The ghetto was in the Jewish Quarter, on the site of the old medieval ghetto, with the Orthodox synagogue as its centerpiece. The Ráczes had been assigned to 20 Szacsvay Street. Éva remarked the "interesting" use of language regarding the new reality: "It occurred to me only when we got to Szacsvay Street that we weren't going to have an apartment, because the commission had said: 'Your place to sleep will be at 20 Szacsvay Street.' It makes a tremendous difference, dear diary, because a normal person has an apartment, while people talk about a 'place to sleep' only in connection with animals. I swear that Ági is right; as far as the Aryans are concerned, we've become like animals."

Ironically, they were now staying with the poor Jews Ági had advised Éva to go see as a cure for her jealousy—and eating like them, their fare consisting of a bowl of beans and seven ounces of bread a day, which they were able to supplement in various ways. A further irony was that the building they moved into had been the residence of the Chief Rabbi of Várad, Éva's uncle, who had died a few years earlier. His granddaughter was Marica, with whom Éva was to share a place on the floor.

The tension of waiting lifted, Éva was relieved, happy. Earlier she had remarked that she did not care how long the war went on with "the Ágis at home." And now, the first night in the ghetto, sharing a room with thirteen others, she said she was happy, and for the same reason: "I cuddled up with Marica, and the two of us—believe it or not, dear diary—were happy. Strange as it seems, everybody belonging to us was here together with us, everybody in the world whom we loved."

Strange, too, was the miraculous recovery of the grandmother. Within two weeks, she became "her old self again," reported Éva. The pressure of an unknown future had driven her mad, and now, within the narrow confines of the ghetto, a certain routine had been reestablished. "She doesn't have any more attacks, and she works somewhere, offering her services to total strangers."

THE GHETTO

But the initial euphoria did not last long. Nagyvárad was one of the worst ghettos in Hungary, because the town's police force was one of the most brutal. The commander of the "ghetto-camp" was Lieutenant Colonel Péterffy. Every house in the ghetto bore a notice signed by him containing no less than eighty rules. There was a ban on leaving one's room and another on leaving the ghetto. The latter was punishable by death. There was to be no contact with the outside. "Any noise, talk, or songs are forbidden. . . . The ghetto must be empty and silent night and day. . . . The Hungarian and German officers are to be saluted bareheaded, and in standing position. This salute is compulsory for women as well." There were seventy-four more.

The ghetto was enclosed by a wooden fence seven

feet tall. The fence ran alongside the house at 20 Szacsvay Street, and Éva used to look outside to see what was happening in Várad—before that, too, became punishable by death, and the windows were whitewashed. No wonder Éva wrote on May 10: "Actually, everything is forbidden, but the most awful thing of all is that the punishment for everything is death. There is no difference between things; no standing in the corner, no spankings, no taking away food, no writing down the declension of irregular verbs one hundred times the way it used to be in school. Not at all: the lightest and heaviest punishment—death. It doesn't actually say that this punishment also applies to children, but I think it does apply to us, too."

But they were still allowed to hear, Éva observed dryly, and one afternoon she and her friend Marica "heard the ice-cream vendor ringing his bell on the other side of the fence. . . . Formerly, whenever I used to hear the ice-cream vendor's bell, I would dash to the gate. Mostly I would ask for a lemon cone." She recalled the time one of the vendor's children had been sick, and she had gone with her grandfather to bring him some medicine free of charge, and that afterward the ice cream man had presented her with a "huge lemon cone and wouldn't take any money for it. . . . Marica and I even told each other how well off the ice-cream man's boy is now, better off than we are; anybody in the world is better off than us, because they all can do whatever they want, and only we are in the ghetto."

Protesting conditions in the Nagyvárad ghetto, the Jewish council of Budapest wrote to Minister of the Interior Andor Jaross:

Subject: The separation of the Jews in Nagyvárad.

We respectfully beg to report to Your Excellency that according to reports in our possession the area allocated to the Jews in Nagyvárad, who number about 30,000 souls, is so limited, that on an average 16 people have to find accommodation in one room. From the sanitary point of view this may constitute a grave danger. We beg leave to mention that the main synagogue of the Congressional Synagogue Council and its offices are not included in the area allocated to the Jews and that consequently the functioning of the Synagogue Council as well as the maintenance of religious services have become impossible. We beg Your Excellency, with deep respect, to deign to order the area allocated to the Jews in Nagyvárad to be enlarged and to make it possible for the Synagogue Council to resume its functions.

The Hungarian authorities were not impressed. Every thing in Nagyvárad had been done "in a humane manner and with regard to all moral factors," Secretary of State László Endre, who could "eat the Jews with paprika," told a newspaper on May 15. "Among other things, we have made it possible for them to use sesame oil for their cooking purposes, so that they are not forced to transgress against their religious laws." On May 17, he and Minister of the Interior Jaross visited Nagyvárad, and Jaross gave a little speech:

Today I saw a new Nagyvárad emerge in the sunshine of May. I saw that here was the new nationalist Nagyvárad, where there are no Jews in the streets. I am convinced that there has been an appropriate segregation of the Jews in this city. Nagyvárad solved this problem, and I notice with satisfaction that solution is in accord with the requirements of the age.

"THERE IS NO NEED IN GERMANY FOR LADIES OF FASHION"

From the moment the Germans came, all Éva could think about was her friend Márta, as she saw the hand that had killed her friend overhead, ready to strike again.

March 26, 1944

Dear diary, until now I didn't want to write about this in you because I tried to put it out of my mind, but ever since the Germans are here, all I think about is Márta. She was also just a girl, and still the Germans killed her. But I don't want them to kill me! I want to be a newspaper photographer, and when I'm twenty-four, I'll marry an Aryan Englishman, or maybe even Pista Vadas.

March 27, 1944

I would be perfectly happy with Uncle Poroszlay in their pigpen or their barn, and would do any kind of work for them, even look after their sheep, just so the Germans shouldn't kill me with a gun as they killed Márta.

March 29, 1944

God, it's true, isn't it, that it is only by accident that You weren't paying attention when they killed Márta, but now You are watching over us?

April 18, 1944

This is the first time I heard Ági say such a thing [that they would all die in Poland]. I mean, so it's true that I'll be taken to Poland, the way Márta was. Maybe I'll also be taken there because I had a red bicycle, like Márta. I know that what I've written here is silly, but believe me, dear diary, I'm afraid that I'm also going out of my mind, like Grandma.

April 19, 1944

I would go . . . to any place in the world where they don't know that I'm Jewish and wherefrom I couldn't be taken to Poland like Márta was.

April 20, 1944

Dear diary, ever since the Germans came here I've often wondered: Had Márta known in Várad what a horrible death was in store for her when she went with her father, would she still have gone? Dear diary,

I admit that I very much want to live, so much so that
if I were given the same choice as Márta, I would stay
even without Papa and without Ági and without anybody at all, because I want to stay alive!

In the ghetto Éva began thinking less but dreaming
more about her friend. Finally, on May 13, in a dream,
she and Márta became one.

I dreamed that I was Márta and I stood in a big field,
bigger than any I had ever seen, and then I realized
that field was Poland. There wasn't a sign of a human
being anywhere, or of a bird, or of any other creature,
and it was still, like that time we were waiting to be
taken to the ghetto. In my dream I was very frightened
by the silence and I started running. Suddenly, that
cross-eyed gendarme who returned the cigarettes to
Ági grabbed me from behind the neck and put his pistol against my nape. The pistol felt cold. I wanted to
scream, but not a sound came out of my throat. I
woke up, and woke up Marica, and told her what an
awful dream I had. Suddenly it occurred to me that is
the way poor Márta must have felt at the moment the
Germans shot her to death! Marica asked me not to
tell her about any more dreams like that. . . .

Staying in a room filled with panic-stricken adults did
nothing to lessen the young girl's anxiety. As ghetto
pharmacists, Grandpa Rácz and his daughter had passes
to leave. Éva overheard her grandfather say that many
people were killing themselves and that he was giving
poison to the older people who asked for it. Ági and

her father also talked about the Dreher Breweries, where Jews were being tortured by functionaries of the Commission for the Unearthing of Jewish Wealth; the torturers wanted to know the whereabouts of the Jews' valuables. The victims were "brought to the hospital bleeding at the mouth and ears, and some of them also with teeth missing and the soles of their feet swollen so that they can't stand."

The head of every household had to go to the Dreher Breweries. The plant was near the ghetto, and to drown out the screaming, the commissioners kept playing the same song over and over, "There Is Just One Girl in the World." Ági and Grandpa Rácz's turn came on May 27. Friends tried to console Éva. "I would see, they wouldn't beat Ági, because Ági didn't live in Várad, and Grandpa would tell them right off that the valuables were with Juszti. . . . A lot I care about the jewelry, I said to them." Two days later Éva was pleased to report that they had let Ági and her grandfather go. "Some policeman in civilian clothes felt sorry for Ági, but I don't know how it happened."

Éva and her family shared the room with "an ugly, small, angry old man," who talked to nobody except Ági. His name was Lusztig, and what Éva heard him say to Ági in the dark made her hair stand on end.

Do you seriously believe, Uncle Lusztig said, that they are going to keep us in this horror called ghetto-camp until the end of the war, and then lead us out beyond the fence in full pomp and circumstance, and announce: Ladies and gentlemen, please throw away your

yellow patches; return to your homes; we give everything back to you, and we beg your pardon for the
slight inconvenience we caused you! No, if you please,
old Lusztig continued, let's speak frankly and plainly.
Do you know where the Jews of Austria are, and
of Germany, and Holland, and Czechoslovakia and
France? . . . Well, if you don't know, I will tell you
now: in Poland. In any case, that is where they were
taken in cattle cars, seventy packed into each car. What
happened to them I do not know, but I can only
guess. . . .

Éva thought Uncle Lusztig was right. All this talk in-
creased her fear of dying. "Altogether, now everybody
says about everything: They will kill you. As if that
weren't the most terrible thing in the world." "I don't
want to die," she cried out time and again, "because
I've hardly lived!" When her father's mother declared
that she wasn't afraid of dying, Éva shot back: "But she
is seventy-two, and I'm only thirteen."

Under the circumstances, the Jews of Nagyvárad
were only too glad to swallow the rumor spread by the
German-Hungarian "dejewification" squad that they
were being taken to work on farms in an area west of
the city, near Lake Balaton. Which was what Ági told
her daughter too. "Oh, I wish only that Ági should be
right, how I would like to harvest!" Éva exclaimed on
May 22. "True, I've never in my life harvested, but I'm
strong, and I could do a good job of harvesting. Even
today Uncle Bándi Kecskeméti [Marica's father] said
that, thank God, neither Marica nor I have become

skinny in the ghetto. Uncle Bándi is a pediatrician, and he can tell, even without scales." "But I don't believe it," declared Éva, referring to the Lake Balaton reports.

May 15 marked the beginning of the deportation of Hungarian Jewry. "Each train will transport 3,000 persons," stated a document issued by the "dejewification" authorities on May 9 and sent to the mayors in ghetto centers. "It will consist of 45 cars, each with 70 persons plus baggage, and two C cars at the front and the back of the train for guards. . . . If necessary, as many as 100 may be put in a car. They can be loaded like sardines, since the Germans require hardy people. Those who cannot take it will perish. There is no need in Germany for ladies of fashion."

The trains waiting to take them bore the slogan "German Worker Resettlement." Between May 24 and June 3, transports left the Nagyvárad ghetto for Auschwitz almost daily. By June 7, thirty-six thousand Jews had been deported and the trains stopped running.

The stories Éva heard from a policeman a few days before deportation confirmed her worst fears. The policeman announced he was quitting the force because of what he had witnessed at the trains. "They stuffed eighty people into each wagon and all they gave them was one pail of water for that many people." "But what is even more awful," exclaimed Éva in disbelief, "is that they bolt the wagons. In this terrible heat we will suffocate in there!"

Such a train pulled up for Éva in the first week of June. The usual procedures were in force. The streets inside and outside the ghetto were blocked off. At nine o'clock an official appeared and told the deportees what to take and how to behave. Then came the hustle and bustle of packing, followed by the rounding up of the sick. At twelve thirty, they marched off, in groups of five hundred, four abreast, as prescribed in the May 9 instructions. By one thirty, the ghetto was no more.

"I CAN'T WRITE ANYMORE, DEAR DIARY"

Éva's last entry is dated May 30. That day she entrusted the diary to her former cook, Mariska, who had been let into the ghetto. Mariska recalled Éva saying, "Take good care of it, Mariska, just like of Mandi [Éva's bird]. Don't cry, Mariska, I'll come home again, I'll survive, because you know how strong I am, Mariska." "Of course, I cried very much," Mariska later wrote to Éva's mother, "and that precious girl even comforted me, saying: 'Don't be upset, you'll be coming back to us yet, you'll see, and I'll go on reading "The Sons of the Stonehearted Man" to you.' "

In her last entry Éva once again raised the image of her friend Márta:

> All I think about is Márta, and I'm afraid that what happened to her is going to happen to us, too. It's no use that everybody says that we're not going to Poland but to Balaton. Even though, dear diary, I don't want to die; I want to live even if it means that I'll be the only person here allowed to stay. I would wait for the

end of the war in some cellar, or on the roof, or in some secret cranny. I would even let the cross-eyed gendarme, the one who took our flour away from us, kiss me, just as long as they didn't kill me, only that they should let me live. . . . Now I see that friendly gendarme has let Mariska come in. I can't write anymore, dear diary, the tears run from my eyes. . . .

Budapest, 1947.

Ági wrote:

Éva reached her destiny on October 17, 1944. She arrived at Auschwitz on June 6, the very day the Allied troops landed in Europe. . . . According to testimonies of surviving eyewitnesses, her vitality did not leave her for a moment, and in spite of the mental and physical agony she had to endure, her physical condition remained comparatively good. According to these testimonies, Marica Kecskeméti, her cousin and friend whom she mentions in her diary, passed away in her arms, but her will to survive did not slacken even then. She fought with all her might to stay alive until that better world, of which we all dreamed in those darkest days of Fascism, was to materialize.

The thirteen-year-old girl had fought for her life against the henchmen of the Third Reich, but the German beast was much too strong for her. . . . Until October 17, Éva lived in Camp C of Auschwitz in the shadow of the heavy clouds of smoke issuing forth from the crematoria. But on that day [Dr. Josef] Mengele carried out his last and largest "selection," apparently in view of the progressing Allied troops. . . . In fact, a good-hearted female doctor was trying to hide my child, but Mengele found her without effort. Éva's feet were full of sore wounds. "Now look at you," Mengele shouted, "you frog, your feet are foul, reeking with puss! Up with you on the truck!" He transported his human material to the crematorium on yellow-colored trucks. Eyewitnesses told me that he himself had pushed her onto the truck. And so Éva's thirteen-year-long life came to an end, in Poland, as she had feared ever since 1941.

Knowing how much Ági loved her husband, Éva wrote on April 5, the day Jews had to start wearing a yellow patch: "All night I thought it would be better to put me out in the street and that some German should give me a good kick in the behind, only that nobody should take Uncle Béla away from Ági."

Éva got her wish, for there were two people who did not get on the last train out of Nagyvárad: Béla and Ági Zsolt. Éva's grandmother had been right: "Where Uncle Béla is concerned, not even Hitler himself can stop Ági." In her final diary entry, Éva mentioned that Ági and Uncle Béla "were whispering something to each other about our staying here in some kind of typhoid hospital, because they plan to say that Uncle Béla has typhoid fever. It's possible, because he had it when he was in the Ukraine."

They succeeded. The ghetto hospital had six patients the day the ghetto was emptied. Also left were "eighteen medical and nursing attendants." According to the introduction to the diary by Dr. Judah Marton, Ági got her husband admitted. They—and we may assume it was Ági, with her knack for "fixing things," who took the lead—then managed to get forged documents. And "one rainy afternoon in June, Béla Zsolt, dressed in a fireman's overalls, walked out the ghetto gate accompanied by Ági, dressed as a Hungarian peasant woman." They reached Budapest and in December arrived in Switzerland.

Ágnes Zsolt was devastated by the death of her daughter—and by guilt. And Juszti was as critical of Ági as she was of herself.

> If there is one thing for which I must blame you, it isn't for having stayed alive while the girl is dead . . . but for not having fought to have Éva with you, even in more modest circumstances. You, who fought so hard for your man when everybody said it was hopeless; you, who in the end succeeded in rescuing him from that horror in which you found yourselves in Várad; and in the end you, who understand people so well, you have an instinct about this sort of thing, you, my Ágike, in this matter you failed! . . .
>
> You are accustomed to hearing the truth from me, even if this truth hurts.

Ági and Béla survived the war and returned to Budapest. Béla Zsolt died in 1949, aged fifty-one. Soon afterward Ági committed suicide. "Her body," writes Dr. Marton, "was found in her house, lying next to a photograph of Éva."

I don't believe that the big men, the politicians and the capitalists alone, are guilty of the war. Oh, no, the little man is just as guilty, otherwise the peoples of the world would have risen in revolt long ago! There's in people simply an urge to destroy, to kill, to murder and rage, and until all mankind, without exception, undergoes a great change, war will be waged, everything that has been built up, cultivated, and grown will be destroyed and disfigured, after which mankind will have to begin all over again.

Anne Frank

"I Must Uphold My Ideals"

The Holocaust knows countless hells but only one shrine. This shrine is located in the center of Amsterdam, and each year thousands of visitors clamber up the ancient building's steep and narrow stairs to have a peek at the cramped quarters where many years ago a young girl kept a diary while hiding from the Nazis. After twenty-five months, the hideout was betrayed and its occupants bundled off to annihilation camps. Only the father of the diarist survived. He and the diary.

Anne's diary is world famous. It has been translated into dozens of languages. It has been made into a movie and a play. It has inspired choreographers, composers, painters, and sculptors, even judges. Teachers use it in their classrooms. Presidents have quoted from it. She's the "world's most famous child."

Anne's fame is well deserved. She was articulate, perceptive, moving, humorous, serious. She was a fine writer. But hers is only one voice, while the victims were many; Anne's experience was unique, but so was that of her peers. The hunted included men, women, and children of all stripes, people with every kind of human response to suffering and terror. Her experience of going into hiding was unusual. Most Jews were holed up in ghettos, at the complete mercy of the killers. Alongside the other four diaries, Anne's looks different than when you read it by itself as the sole voice of the Holocaust. Sharing the stage makes her more human. Like David, Yitzhak, Moshe, and Éva, she was scared, vulnerable, and fighting with all of her heart to survive.

A PAMPERED LIFE

Anne, the second child of Otto and Edith Frank, was born on June 12, 1929, in Frankfurt, Germany, having been preceded by her sister, Margot, in 1926. Although they were well-to-do, the Franks were nowhere as rich as their immediate ancestors. Otto Frank was the son of a banker and had had "a real little rich boy's upbringing," Anne wrote on May 8, 1944, "parties every week, balls, festivities, beautiful girls, dinners, a large home, etc., etc." Her mother had been wealthy as well, she went on, "and we often listen open-mouthed to stories of engagements parties of two hundred and fifty people, private balls, and dinners." "One certainly could not call us rich now," Anne concluded her brief history of the family's past and present fortunes, noting how hard her father had laughed the day before when "for the first time in his fifty-five years, he scraped out the frying pan at table."

Anne's father grew up in Frankfurt, a city with a reputation as an "island of tolerance." Otto Frank could not remember ever having encountered anti-Semitism in his youth. That would soon change. The Franks continued to live in Frankfurt until Anne was four. The year was 1933 and Hitler was in power. On April 1 the Nazis launched a campaign to boycott Jewish shops, and a week later there were laws banning Jews from the civil service and other areas of German life. Like many German Jews, Mr. Frank decided it was time to leave, crossing the border to explore business opportunities in Holland. The rest of the family soon joined him in Amsterdam, where he had started a firm supplying pectin to factories making jam. But seven years later Hitler followed in their path, and the good times were over. Like David's in Krajno and Éva's in Nagyvárad, Anne's pen registered the Nazi shadow as it passed across her life. The first shadows were cast by regulations and decrees, dos and don'ts. In October 1941, the Frank girls were forced to transfer to a Jewish high school. Summarizing the period leading up to their going into hiding, Anne wrote:

> Anti-Jewish decrees followed each other in quick succession. Jews must wear a yellow star, Jews must hand in their bicycles, Jews are banned from trams and are forbidden to drive, Jews are only allowed to do their shopping between three and five o'clock and then only

in shops which bear the placard "Jewish Shop." Jews must be indoors by eight o'clock and cannot even sit in their own gardens after that hour. Jews are forbidden to visit cinemas and other places of entertainment. Jews may not take part in public sports. Swimming baths, tennis courts, hockey fields, and other sports grounds are all prohibited to them. Jews may not visit Christians. Jews must go to Jewish schools, and many more restrictions of a similar kind.

Anne's parents were decent, law-abiding, respectful of others, conventional. Like all parents, they wanted what was best for their children. Uncharacteristically, though, they considered their daughters' happiness to be more important than good grades. Margot and Anne grew up as moderns: independent, free-thinking, tolerant. "As for discipline—'The system is patience,' " Mr. Frank informed a "family-life expert" in a postwar interview. "Anne was sometimes difficult," and when she was little, they would occasionally give her "a quick spank," he confided.

Anne and her sister were pampered. In the last photograph taken of them before leaving for Holland, they wore furs, gloves, kneesocks, patent leather shoes, and hats. A picture in Margot's photo album has her sitting upright on a bed cuddling a stuffed animal and wearing dark aviator goggles to protect her eyes against the light of an ultraviolet sun lamp. When the family was taken by train to Westerbork, the camp in Holland from which they would be deported to Auschwitz, a fellow deportee "was amazed how well-dressed and well-cared for the Frank girls looked." The day they were dispatched to Auschwitz, they "looked as if they were going on a skiing holiday," recalled Janny Brilleslijper. "They had no idea what was in store for them."

The fussing and fretting accompanied the girls into hiding. Every book Anne read had to be approved, though the rules were not very strict, she admitted. Nor was she allowed to have salt. As she got older, Anne grew tired of the kissie-kissie stuff and the cute little nicknames. "I think it's awfully annoying, the way they ask if you've got a headache, or whether you don't feel well, if you happened to give a sigh and put your hand to your head!" she quoted Margot as saying. In the course of writing about her "good and bad side," which happens to be the very last diary entry, Anne mentioned that every time she departed ever so slightly from the norm, when she was serious and quiet, for example, "my own family, who are sure to think I'm ill, make me swallow pills for headaches and nerves, feel my head and my neck to see whether I'm running a temperature, ask if I'm constipated and criticize me for being in a bad mood."

FATHER AND DAUGHTER

Anne was crazy about her father, "good old Pim," "the dearest darling of a father I have ever seen." She crawled into his bed when she was frightened. They prayed together. She cut his hair. He talked to her about sex, menstruation—things she would have preferred to learn from her mother, she confessed.

Anne's relationship with her father was not without its problems, however. She complained that her father always talked to her as though she were a child going through a difficult phase, forgetting that she was getting older. One of her housemates was Peter Van Daan, who was a few years older than herself. When she began spending a lot of time in Peter's room, Pim reproached her and asked her to stop fooling around. This triggered a letter in which she expressed her frustration. "Since we've been here, from July 1942 until a few weeks ago, I can assure you that I haven't had an easy time," Anne wrote on May 5, 1944.

If you only knew how I cried in the evening, how unhappy I was, how lonely I felt, then you would understand that I want to go upstairs! . . . I've shed many a tear before I became as independent as I am now. You can laugh at me and not believe me, but that can't harm me. I know that I am a separate individual and I don't feel in the least bit responsible to any one of you. . . . When I was in difficulties you all closed your eyes and stopped up your ears and didn't help me; on the contrary, I received nothing but warnings not to be so boisterous. I was only boisterous so as not to be miserable all the time. I played a comedy for a year and a half, day in, day out, I never grumbled, never lost my cue, nothing like that—and now, now the battle is over. I have won! I am independent both in mind and in body. I don't need a mother anymore, for all this conflict has made me strong.

She tucked the letter into her father's pocket, and waited. After leaving it there, she felt guilty, thinking she had been unfair to him. Two days later, the two got together to clear the air; "the good Pim" forgave her and both had a good cry.

But the letter and the cry had not, it seems, solved the problem. Mr. Frank's ideas on child rearing had a textbook quality, and he did not substantially change the way he related to his daughter. On July 15 she again complained that her mother and father did not understand her, despite having done everything "parents could do." "And yet I've felt so terribly lonely for a long time, so left out, neglected, and misunderstood." She further complained that her father had tried to curb her rebelliousness and spoken to her in patronizing platitudes, twaddling on about "symptoms of age," "other girls," and how it would all pass of itself. Although Pim had demonstrated that he trusted her and made her feel confident about herself, he did not really know what she was about, Anne continued. All she wanted was to be treated as Anne-the-individual, but of that he simply seemed incapable.

Anne mentioned a curious thing about her father— that she did not really know him, for he never spoke about himself. Which was the reason why she could not tell him what she was really thinking. On his part, Otto Frank stated after the war that he had no idea his daughter had such deep thoughts, that he got to know her only through the diary.

Despite Anne's sometimes stormy relationship with her father, she could always be sure of one thing: his love. Éva was less fortunate; she felt she was competing with her stepfather for the love that she craved from her mother. David was not old enough to realize that the beating he got from his father had nothing to do with lack of feeling for him, as he thought. David, Éva, and Anne experienced emotional pressures that arise in any family. Their conflict was part of the natural process of growing up. Under the Nazis these feelings were pushed to extremes. Growing pains don't stop just because there is a war going on and life hangs in the balance.

LIFE IN HIDING

For much of the time life in the annex was a series of greater and lesser vexations: rotting potatoes, lights that failed, beans that spilled, clothes that didn't fit, doctors' visits that had to wait, and so forth. But these were only "things." Far more troublesome were people problems. Because Anne was a terrific writer, it is easy to forget that her journal is a distillation of thousands of hours spent under prisonlike conditions. In addition to the run-ins with her parents, especially with her mother, for whom she expressed genuine aversion, Anne reported frequently on the penny-ante tortures she had to put up with every day: annoying adults; their incessant whining, bickering, and endless chatter about politics, food, and sleep; their strange capacity to find the same old jokes amusing or, alternatively, to sit glued to the radio listening to broadcasts endlessly repeating themselves, not to mention their irritating and disgusting habits, such as Dussel's snoring and her father's delight in adolescent bathroom humor. No wonder she yearned to be alone, for privacy and freedom of movement.

Yet compared with Éva, Yitzhak, and David, Anne led an almost "normal" life. She had books checked out from the library. She continued to receive fan magazines and to cut out pictures of her favorite movie stars. She experimented with different hairdos. In the early part of captivity, she felt rather like she was "on vacation in a very peculiar boardinghouse," and as late as May 3, 1944, she referred to her situation as "amusing," "a dangerous adventure, romantic and interesting at the same time."

The occupants of Prinsengracht 263 tried very hard to stick to their prewar routine. They had coffee at four, celebrated birthdays and various holidays, and continued to read Schiller and Goethe, eighteenth-century German writers whose works championed individual freedom and universal brotherhood.

Though it might have been reassuring, there was a flip side to clinging to set ways in the face of "the ever-approaching thunder." Most parents tried to find a refuge for their children away from cities, on farms, and in small towns, where they were less likely to be discovered, often deliberately separating them to maximize the chances that some might survive. By contrast, the Franks had opted to keep the family together in a warehouse where people worked in the daytime and burglars came by at night.

When Anne turned fourteen, on June 12, 1943, her birthday was celebrated as though they were still living in freedom. There was a poem by Pim, and she "got very nice things," including a big book about Greek mythology, her favorite subject, and candy. The following year she received five volumes of art history, a botany book, underwear, two belts, a handkerchief, yogurt, jam, honeycakes, flowers, and so forth. Neither David Rubinowicz nor Moshe Flinker mentioned birthdays. Yitzhak Rudashevski remembered his only after it had already passed, using the occasion to take stock and to plan his future course.

All things considered, life in the "secret annex" was a good deal better than in the ghettos of Vilna, Bodzentyn, and Nagyvárad. Anne had enough to eat, even if the food was not always up to snuff. (Once, she had had so many strawberries she could not stand the sight of them.) Much of the time life in the hideout was simply boring.

Anne was not unaware of her good fortune. Like Moshe, whose situation most resembled hers, she felt guilty. "Cycling, dancing, whistling, looking out into the world, feeling young, to know that I am free— that's what I long for; still, I mustn't show it. . . ." Everybody in the annex was so self-centered, she complained, not excluding herself. Instead of saving "every penny to help other people, and save what is left from the wreckage after the war," they talked about the new shoes and clothes they were going to buy.

Anne had a probing, restless, inquisitive mind. Being shut in could not stop her from developing, and probably accelerated the process. As she argued in the letter to her father that she later regretted writing: "You can't and mustn't regard me as fourteen, for all these troubles have made me older. . . ."

ANNE'S MANY SIDES

Perhaps the most immediate benefit of life in hiding was the opportunity to give her penetrating mind free rein. Whether exploring the cause of female oppression, the roots of war, or the meaning of love, Anne is not bashful about giving her opinions, which she does in a language that is both entertaining and gripping.

March 2, 1944

> *Love, what is love? I believe love is something that can't really be put into words. Love is understanding someone, caring for someone, sharing their ups and downs. And in the long run that also means physical love, you have shared something, given something away and received something, no matter whether you are married or unmarried, or whether you are with child or not. It doesn't matter in the least if you've lost your honor, as long as you know that someone will stand by you, will understand you for the rest of your life, someone you won't have to share with anyone else!* [Anne's emphasis]

May 3, 1944

I don't believe that the big men, the politicians and the capitalists alone, are guilty of the war. Oh, no, the little man is just as guilty, otherwise the peoples of the world would have risen in revolt long ago! There's in people simply an urge to destroy, to kill, to murder and rage, and until all mankind, without exception, undergoes a great change, war will be waged, everything that has been built up, cultivated, and grown will be destroyed and disfigured, after which mankind will have to begin all over again.

June 13, 1944

A question that has been raised more than once and that gives me no inner peace is why did so many nations in the past, and often still now, treat women as inferior to men? Everyone can agree how unjust this is, but that is not enough for me, I would also like to know the cause of this great injustice.

Anne was at her best, however, when analyzing herself, monitoring her inner states as closely as Yitzhak tracked the progress of the Soviet Army and Moshe watched for signs from God to save His people. Of all the diarists, Anne is by far the most introspective. "Now I look back at that Anne," she wrote on March 7, 1944, referring to an earlier Anne, "as an amusing, but very superficial girl, who has nothing to do with the Anne of today."

I look upon my life till the New Year, as it were, through a powerful magnifying glass. The sunny life at home, then coming here in 1942, the sudden change, the quarrels, the bickering, I couldn't understand it, I was taken by surprise, and the only way I could keep up some bearing was by being impertinent.

The first half of 1943: my fits of crying, the loneliness, how I slowly began to see all my faults and shortcomings, which are so great and which seemed much greater then. During the day I deliberately talked about anything and everything that was farthest from my thoughts, tried to draw Pim to me, but couldn't. Alone, I had to face the difficult task of changing myself, to stop the everlasting reproaches, which were so oppressive and which reduced me to such terrible despondency.

Things improved slightly in the second half of the year, I became a young woman and was treated more like a grown-up. I started to think, and write stories, and came to the conclusion that the others no longer had the right to throw me about like an india-rubber ball. I wanted to change in accordance with my own desires. But *one* thing that struck me even more was when I realized that not even Daddy would never become my confidant over everything. I didn't want to trust anyone but myself anymore.

August 1, 1944

I've already told you before that I have, as it were, a dual personality. One half embodies my exuberant cheerfulness, making fun of everything, my high-spiritedness, and above all, the way I take everything lightly. . . . This side is usually lying in wait and pushes away the other, which is much better, deeper, and purer. . . .

I am awfully scared that everyone who knows me

as I always am will discover that I have another side, a finer and better side. I'm afraid they'll laugh at me, think I'm ridiculous and sentimental, not take me seriously.

ANNE, DAVID, YITZHAK, MOSHE, AND ÉVA

Different people, different diaries. David, Yitzhak, Moshe, Éva, and Anne had different sets of parents, who made their homes in different parts of Europe. They differed in character, temperament, and interests. Moreover, they varied in age. A year can make a big difference in a teenager's life. David had not even turned thirteen when he recorded his first diary entry and was eight weeks away from turning fifteen when the diary breaks off. Éva and Anne were thirteen when they started theirs, but while Anne kept hers for more than two years, Éva's spanned less than four months. Yitzhak was thirteen when the Germans invaded and he started writing, fifteen and a half when he stopped. Moshe had just turned sixteen when he wrote his first entry and kept at it for almost a year. Anne, Moshe, David, and Yitzhak were able to keep their diaries for a long time, but only in Anne is there noticeable internal growth and development, as she is the first to tell us.

Situation and place had a lot to do with that. David in the Polish countryside and Yitzhak in Vilna were simply too busy dodging the "Nazi dogs." Besides, Yitzhak was committed to a cause larger than himself, as was Moshe, whose utter devotion to his people in need and religious probing left room for little else. And Éva, Éva never had a chance. Unlike David, Éva, and Yitzhak, Anne was not immediately threatened and had plenty of time to think, and so could freely write and reflect on God, human nature, the place of women, male-female relations, family. When a minister speaking on Radio Orange, the voice of the Dutch government in exile, urged people to record their experiences for possible inclusion in a postwar collection, she got excited and sat down to polish her prose. She planned to publish a book based on her experiences in the hideout, using the diary she called Kitty as a source. In addition to the diary, she was writing short stories and thinking about placing one with a publisher under an assumed name.

What reading was to Yitzhak and God to Moshe, writing was to Anne—"the finest thing I have." Writing kept her going: "I can shake off everything if I write; my sorrows disappear, my courage is reborn. . . ." She used her diary as a confessional and poured into it all her "joys, sorrows, and contempt." "Anyone who doesn't write doesn't know how wonderful it is. . . ." Without it, she said, she would suffocate. It was as a writer that she envisaged her future. The diary was the first thing she packed when they moved to the annex. When burglars were mucking around in the warehouse and someone suggested burning the diary because it would incriminate them if they were caught, Anne burst out: "Not my diary; if my diary goes, I go with it!"

Anne Frank shared with the other teenage writers a passion for learning. "The only way to take one's mind off it all is to study, and I do a lot of that." "Oh, something else, the Bible," she exclaimed on May 11, 1944, "how long is it going to take before I meet the bathing Suzannah? And what do they mean by the guilt of Sodom and Gomorrah? Oh, there is still such a terrible lot to find out and to learn." One day Anne had a "pile of work" to get through, which included finishing the first part of the biography of Galileo, copying and memorizing three pages of difficult vocabulary extracted from recent reading, working out the genealogies of members of the royal families found in the biography of Charles V she had just completed, and getting a handle on the Greeks Theseus, Oedipus, Peleus, Orpheus, Jason, and Hercules.

Anne considered herself a prime example of the human capacity for self-improvement. Having cooled on Peter because of what she considered his fatal character flaw—lack of backbone—she mused:

> We all live, but we don't know the why or the wherefore. We all live with the object of being happy, our lives are all different yet the same. We three [Margot, Peter, and herself] have been brought up in good circles, we have the chance to learn, the possibility of attaining something, we have all reason to hope for much happiness, but . . . we must earn it for ourselves. And that is never easy. You must work and do good, not be lazy and gamble, if you wish to earn happiness. Laziness may *appear* attractive, but work *gives* satisfaction.

Unlike Peter, Anne was totally focused and set high goals for herself. She dreamed of fame—"I want to go on living even after my death!"—and criticized her mother and Margot. Anne could not see herself as "merely a housewife." She yearned to go to Paris and London, learn the languages, study art history. She wanted to meet interesting people and wear nice dresses, and "a little money" wouldn't hurt, either. "Compare that with Margot, who wants to be a midwife in Palestine!" Anne vowed that she'd "work in the world and for mankind!" But unlike Yitzhak Rudashevski and Moshe Flinker, who made similar commitments, she did not say how.

Anne's breezy writing style and cheery disposition make it easy to forget that the "secret redoubt" was a pressure cooker bursting with tension. The lodgers quarreled, bombers roared, burglars prowled, and the specter of discovery hovered. "At night, when I'm in bed," Anne wrote on November 8, 1943, "I see myself alone in a dungeon, without Mummy and Daddy. Sometimes I wander by the roadside, or our 'Secret Annex' is on fire, or they come and take us away at night. I see everything as if it is actually taking place, and this gives me the feeling that it may all happen to me very soon!" She was well aware that the "little piece of blue heaven" that was the hiding place was under siege by "heavy black rain clouds" that were coming closer and closer and threatened to crush them. No wonder she took tranquilizers every day "against fear and depression."

But the tension in the "house in back" was very different from that experienced by the young writers in

Vilna, Nagyvárad, and Krajno. Theirs was the tension that paralyzes and breaks people—as in Nagyvárad, where a Hungarian policeman charged with overseeing the deportations watched in disbelief as Jews let themselves be stuffed eighty to a wagon without a whimper. "The policeman says that he doesn't understand these Jews," reported Éva; "not even the children cried; all of them were like zombies; like robots." In the Amsterdam refuge, persecution, destruction, and death were shadows hovering offstage.

Still, the news that penetrated the annex was horrible enough. The makeshift quarters that lay concealed at the top of the narrow stairs behind the fake bookcase had one great merit—its only merit: It kept the real world out, which, after all, was the whole point. The outside hardly entered, except as filtered through the "illegal" broadcasts of the BBC and Radio Orange in London and the small but devoted group of friends who looked after the Franks. What Anne learned about Westerbork, for example, made her tremble with fear. The human warehouse on the Dutch heath conjured up visions of the fate that would be hers, if discovered: cattle cars, shaved heads, prisoners dumped pell-mell in large barracks. "If it is as bad as this in Holland," she wrote in October 1942, "whatever will it be like in those distant and barbarous regions they are sent to? We assume that most of them are murdered. The English radio speaks of their being gassed." A month later:

In the evening, when it's dark, I often see rows of good, innocent people accompanied by crying children, walking on and on, in the charge of a couple of these chaps, bullied and knocked about until they almost drop. No one is spared—old people, babies, expectant mothers, the sick—each and all join in the march of death. How fortunate we are here, so well cared for and undisturbed. We wouldn't have to worry about all this misery were it not that we are so anxious about all those dear to us whom we can no longer help. I feel wicked sleeping in a warm bed, while my dearest friends have been knocked down or have fallen into a gutter somewhere out in the cold night.

But unlike, say, David or Yitzhak, Anne was in a position to avert her eyes, while her temperament, in contrast to Moshe's, enabled her to turn the horror off and to pull the blankets over her head. Anne felt it was no use to turn the hideout into a "Secret Annex of Gloom." "Must I keep thinking about those other people, whatever I am doing?" she asked herself, referring to the Jews who had been deported. "And if I want to laugh about something, should I stop myself quickly and feel ashamed that I am cheerful? Ought I then to cry the whole day long? No, that I can't do. Besides, in time this gloom will wear off." Having witnessed a procession of hungry and ill-clad children, she commented: "I could go on for hours about all the suffering the war has brought, but then I would only make myself more dejected." After hearing that Holland was to be emptied of Jews, province by province, she remarked: "These wretched people are sent to filthy slaughterhouses like a herd of sick, neglected cattle. But

I won't talk about it, I only get nightmares from such thoughts."

One nightmare she could not shake concerned her friend Hanneli (Lies) Goslar. Anne felt doubly guilty, because she believed she had done Lies wrong by trying to steal one of her girlfriends. She imagined her friend dressed in rags, skinny, looking at her reproachfully with eyes that implored: "Rescue me from this hell!" "And I cannot help her, I can only look on, how others suffer and die, and can only pray to God to send her back to us." "Oh, God," Anne continued, "that I should have all I could wish for and she, that she should be seized by such a terrible fate. I am not more virtuous than she; she, too, wanted to do what was right, why should I be chosen to live and she probably to die? What was the difference between us? Why are we so far from each other now?"

Anne's lament was one all of the diarists could make, for there wasn't one among them who didn't mourn a special friend. Anne's Hanneli was Éva's Márta, Yitzhak's Benkye Nayer, Moshe's Finkel, and David's former neighbor's daughter, "a girl as pretty as a picture." The murder of friends left gaping wounds that never closed. Of all the senseless suffering thrown up by the war, nothing seemed to make less sense to them than the death of their friends. And nothing caused them more anguish.

Thus to Anne, Hanneli was "a symbol . . . of the sufferings of all my girlfriends and all Jews." She realized that Hanneli could easily have been her, and wondered why, then, she so often still felt unhappy.

"Shouldn't I always be glad, contented, and happy, except when I think about her and her companions in distress?" She berated herself for having fallen short—"I am selfish and cowardly"—and for being "safely" tucked away in the hideout. She had the most terrible dreams, and at times her fear was so great as to make her want to scream out loud. "If you think of your fellow creatures, then you only want to cry, you could really cry the whole day long. The only thing to do is to pray that God will perform a miracle and save some of them. And I hope that I am doing that enough!"

"WE WILL ALWAYS REMAIN JEWS"

The Franks were not religious but did believe in God. "Whether you are a Jew or a Christian, there is only one God," Mr. Frank told the first person he met when he got out of Auschwitz. "Only the paths to him are a little different." Anne's father rejected the first stage adaptation of the diary, by Meyer Levin, because it nonsensically presented the Franks as Orthodox Jews.

Yet Judaism meant a great deal to Anne, and she had absorbed a good deal of it in a nonreligious form: the idea, for example, of history as a progressive, meaningful sequence of events, with a beginning, middle, and an end—a happy end. A burglary scare having reminded her that they were marked Jews "without any rights," she reflected:

Sometime this terrible war will be over. Surely the time will come when we are people again, and not just Jews. Who has inflicted this upon us? Who has made us Jews different from all other people? Who has allowed us to suffer so terribly up till now? It is God that has made us as we are, but it will be God, too, who will raise us up again. If we bear all this suffering and if there are still Jews left, when it is over, then Jews, instead of being doomed, will be held up as an example. Who knows, it might even be our religion from which the world and all peoples learn good, and for that reason and that reason only do we have to suffer now. We can never become just Netherlanders, or just English, or representative of any country for that matter, we will always remain Jews, but we want to, too. . . .

God has never deserted our people. Right through the ages there have been Jews, through all the ages they have had to suffer, but it has made them strong, too; the strong will remain and never go under!

Anne's conception of Judaism was quite different from Moshe's. Where Moshe had no interest in spreading Judaism, Anne professed to be a respecter of all religions. She hated it when Peter made fun of Jesus Christ and took the name of God in vain. She thought people were better off having a religion because "it keeps a person on the right path." For Anne, religion had nothing to do with fear of God, or heaven and hell, but "upholding one's honor and conscience." Every evening before falling asleep, people should take stock of their actions that day and decide whether they

had been "good or "bad." That was how people could
gradually improve themselves, she said. "Anyone can
do this, it costs nothing and is certainly very helpful.
Whoever doesn't know it must learn and find by experience that: 'A quiet conscience makes one strong!' "
Anne herself habitually ended her evening prayers
thanking God "for all that is good and dear and beautiful." She fervently wished that after the war Jews
would be thought of not just as Jews but as human beings, too.

In the first months of 1944, the closing words of the
nightly ritual began to take on a special significance:
"All that is good and dear and beautiful" must have included Peter—"love, the future, the happiness." It was
with him that she spent "the most wonderful evening
I have ever had in the 'Secret Annex,' " the evening of
March 19, 1944. Anne's evening to remember was not
at all like Yitzhak's, whose most beautiful evening was
a club party given over to eating baked pudding,
drinking coffee, talking, singing, and reciting. Hers
took place in the loft, standing in the twilight talking
to Peter by the open window in the attic, she on the
right side, he on the left:

> We told each other so much, so very very much, that
> I can't repeat it all, but it was lovely. . . . We talked
> about how we neither of us confide in our parents,
> and how his parents would have loved to have his con-
> fidence, but that he didn't wish it. How I cry my heart
> out in bed, and he goes up into the loft and swears.
> How Margot and I really only know each other well

for a little while, but that, even so, we don't tell each other everything, because we are always together. Over every imaginable thing—oh, he was just as I thought! Then we talked about 1942, how different we were then. We just don't recognize ourselves as the same people anymore. How we simply couldn't bear each other in the beginning. He thought I was just too talkative and unruly, and I soon came to the conclusion that I'd no time for him. I didn't understand why he didn't flirt with me, but now I'm glad. He also mentioned how much he isolated himself from us all. I said there was not much difference between my noise and his silence. That I love peace and quiet too, and have nothing for myself alone, except my diary. . . . That I understand his reserve now and his relationship with his parents, and how I would love to be able to help him.

"You always do help me," he said. "How?" I asked, very surprised. "By your cheerfulness." That was certainly the loveliest thing he said. It was wonderful, he must have grown to love me as a friend, and that is enough for the time being. I am so grateful and happy, I just can't find the words.

Peter was right: Anne had a sunny disposition. "I'm not rich in money or worldly goods, I'm not beautiful, intelligent, or smart," Anne wrote on March 25, 1944, "but I am and I shall be happy! I have a happy nature, I like people, I'm not distrustful and would like to see all of them happy with me."

Happiness and optimism go hand in hand. Anne's father's positive attitude seems to have rubbed off on his younger daughter. How can you get over feeling low? Think about all the misery in the world and count your lucky stars, Anne's mother advised. But Anne thought differently: "I don't see how Mummy's idea can be right, because then how are you supposed to behave if you go through the misery yourself? Then you are lost. On the contrary, I've found that there is always some beauty left—in nature, sunshine, freedom, in yourself; these can all help you. Look at these things, then you find yourself again, and God, and then you regain your balance. And whoever is happy will make others happy too. He who has courage and faith will never perish in misery!"

Anne's optimism was very different from Yitzhak's. While Yitzhak believed that people could be programmed to be good by creating favorable social and economic conditions, culminating in the establishment of a communist paradise, Anne saw her fellow human beings as capable of self-improvement through individual effort and of taking control over their own lives. Evil in Anne's view was an aberration, a temporary relapse into barbarism. It would be hard to imagine Yitzhak looking into the heavens and coming away convinced that everything would turn out all right, without struggle, painlessly. It would be altogether impossible for Moshe Flinker. When Moshe looked out of the window he saw the "sky covered with bloody clouds." Different diarists, different beliefs.

"I STILL BELIEVE PEOPLE ARE GOOD AT HEART"

On August 4, 1944, a car stopped in front of the building with the hideout. Four men got out and entered the premises. They reemerged with the eight "lawbreakers" in tow. Soon these were on their way to Westerbork, the transit camp in Holland from which they would be dispatched to the Auschwitz death camp. At the end of October, Anne and her sister Margot were "evacuated" from the killing center and shipped to Bergen-Belsen in northern Germany, where both died toward the end of the winter of 1945, from typhus and starvation.

Two weeks before she was hauled from the annex, Anne penned the words that have stuck, the words with which both the play and the film based on the diary end: "It's really a wonder that I haven't dropped all my ideals," she wrote on July 15, 1944, "because they seem so absurd and impossible to carry out. Yet I keep them, because in spite of everything I still believe that people are really good at heart."

That dream lived on in a crowded loft, with the sound of the Wester Tower, Anne's "faithful friend," to remind her every fifteen minutes that things could not possibly be as bad as they seemed (the bells stopped pealing in March 1943). But they were, and we will never know whether Anne was able to hold on to her beliefs in Auschwitz and Bergen-Belsen.

Though the Nazis killed them all, Anne, David, Yitzhak, Moshe, and Éva left diaries that demonstrate the endurance and beauty of the human spirit—"in spite of everything." All five stand as a testimony and an inspiration, as if to urge us never to give up hope, and to live up to what Anne wrote in her very next paragraph:

I simply can't build up my hopes on a foundation consisting of confusion, misery, and death. I see the world gradually being turned into a wilderness, I hear the ever-approaching thunder, which will destroy us too, I can feel the sufferings of millions, and yet, if I look up into the heavens, I think that it will all come right, that this cruelty too will end, and that peace and tranquillity will return again. In the meantime, I must uphold my ideals, for perhaps the time will come when I shall be able to carry them out.

NOTES

INTRODUCTION

Page 3: Abraham Souckever [Sutzkever], *Ghetto de Vilna*, trans. Ch. Brenasin (Sens, France: Copped, 1950), 132.

Page 6: H. Rauschning, *Hitler Speaks* (London: T. Butterfield, 1940), 247.

Page 7: For translation of the diary I've relied on *The Diary of Anne Frank: The Critical Edition* by Anne Frank. Copyright © 1986 by Anne Frank-Fonds, Basel, Switzerland. Used by permission of Doubleday, a division of Bantam-Doubleday-Dell Publishing Group, Inc. That translation is the one prepared by Mrs. B. M. Mooyaart-Doubleday (first published in 1952). The translator of parts not previously translated is Arnold J. Pomerans. All the quotations cited in the introduction are from this source unless otherwise noted.

Page 10: Randolph L. Braham, *The Politics of Genocide: The Holocaust in Hungary*, vol. II (New York: Columbia University Press, 1981), 691.

CHAPTER 1: DAVID RUBINOWICZ

Page 13: "Das Diensttagebuch des deutschen Generalgouverneurs in Polen 1939–1945," *Quellen und Darstellungen zur Zeitgeschichte,* vol. 20. Edited by Werner Präg and Wolfgang Jacobmeyer. (Stuttgart: Deutsche Verlags-Anstalt,

1975), 53. "Speech by Hans Frank on the Extermination of the Jews, December 16, 1941," in *Documents of the Holocaust: Selected Sources on the Destruction of the Jews of Germany, Austria, Poland, and the Soviet Union*, ed. Yitzhak Arad, Yisrael Gutman, and Abraham Margoliot (Jerusalem: Yad Vashem, 1981), 247–48.

Page 14: All quotes are taken from the English edition of the diary: *The Diary of David Rubinowicz*, trans. Derek Bowman (Edinburgh: William Blackwood, 1981). In quoting, I have taken the liberty to "Americanize" some of the vocabulary. Thus "truck" instead of "lorry" and "sleigh" or "cart" instead of "sledge." All quotations cited in Chapter 1 are from this source unless otherwise noted.

Page 14: Facsimile of David's report card in the Polish edition of the diary, *Pamietnik Dawida Rubinowicza* (Warsaw: Ksiazka i Wiedza, 1960), 85–87.

Page 14: Some of the facts of David's life and that of his family can be found in Derek Bowman's introduction to the English version of the diary, which in turn is based on Maria Jarochowska's introduction to the German edition: *Das Tagebuch des David Rubinowicz*, trans. Stanislaw Zylinski (Berlin: Kinderbuchverlag, 1961).

Page 37: See Adam Rutkowski, "The further trials of the Jewish population of Bodzentyn," in *Dagboek van David Rubinowicz*, trans. H. P. van den Aardweg (Amsterdam: A. J. H. Strengholt, 1960), 91–94.

CHAPTER 2: YITZHAK RUDASHEVSKI

Page 41: The red flag was the communist flag. In 1917 communist revolutionaries came to power in Russia, setting an example that followers of the international workers' movement sought to duplicate in other countries, including Germany. After Germany's defeat in World War I, communists there succeeded for a brief period in raising the red flag in various parts of the country before being overthrown by returning troops.

Page 42: Yitskhok Rudashevski, *The Diary of the Vilna Ghetto, June 1941–April 1943* (Israel: Ghetto Fighters' House and Hakibbutz Hameuchad Publishing House, 1973). I have used the English edition, which, in turn, is based on the original Yiddish manuscript and the 1968 Hebrew Edition with its extensive set of notes. The editor of the English version, Percy Matenko, incorporated the introduction to the Hebrew-language edition by Tsvi Shner and expanded on the notes. The only liberty I have taken is to transliterate Yitskhok to Yitzhak, which is the more familiar English spelling. For some of my information, I have relied on the excellent notes to the

English version. All quotations cited in Chapter 2 are based on the English edition unless otherwise noted.

Page 44: Abraham A. Souckever [Sutzkever], *Ghetto de Vilna,* 112.

Page 45: Marc Dvorjetski, *Ghetto à l'est,* trans. Arnold Mandel (Paris: Robert Marin, 1950), 17. In addition to Yitzhak, there were many other chroniclers of the events in the Vilna ghetto. Some, like Marc Dvorjetski (Mark Dvorzhetski) and Abraham Sutzkever, recorded their memories after the war, while Yitzhak Rudashevski and Herman Kruk kept a contemporary record. The latter kept the most complete record in what has to be the most percipient diary of that time. In the course of this chapter, Kruk and others will be used to complement the information in Rudashevski's diary. Kruk's diary is called *Togbukh fun vilner geto [Diary of the Vilna Ghetto],* (New York: Yidisher Visnshaftlekher Institut [YIVO], 1961).

Page 46: Dvorjetski, *Ghetto à l'est,* 199; Souckever, *Ghetto de Vilna,* 9.

Page 48: Kruk, *Togbukh,* 8–9.

Page 49: Text of the notice, in Dvorjetski, *Ghetto à l'est,* 38.

Page 50: Kruk, *Togbukh,* 51. Thursday, September 4, 1941; and September 4 and 5, 51–58.

Page 52: Statistics on ghetto population, from Yitzhak Arad, *Ghetto in Flames: The Struggle and Destruction of the Jews in Vilna in the Holocaust* (Jerusalem: Yad Vashem, 1980), 113.

Page 53: Arad, *Ghetto in Flames,* 145–47.

Page 54: Dvorjetski, *Ghetto à l'est,* 81, 89, 96, 118; Souckever, *Ghetto de Vilna,* 57–58.

Page 57: *Encyclopedia of the Holocaust* (New York: Macmillan Publishing Co., 1990). The entry gives an excellent chronology of the various "actions" of the first half year.

Page 58: Dvorjetski, *Ghetto à l'est,* 187, 189.

Page 59: Souckever, *Ghetto de Vilna,* 52.

Page 59: Souckever, *Ghetto de Vilna,* 95–96, 123, 158–59.

Page 62: The complete text of Yitzhak's speech can be found in Appendix A of the English translation, pp. 141–43.

Page 64: Souckever, *Ghetto de Vilna,* 114–16.

Page 70: Quoted in Yitzhak Arad, "The Judenraete [Jewish councils] in the Lithuanian Ghettos of Kovno and Vilna," in *Patterns of Jewish Leadership in Nazi Europe 1933–1945,* Proceedings of the Third Yad Vashem International Historical Conference, Jerusalem, April 4–7, 1977 (Jerusalem: Yad Vashem, 1979), 105.

Page 71: Quoted in Arad, *Ghetto in Flames,* 323.

Page 76: Arad, *Ghetto in Flames,* 231. See also the film *Partisans of Vilna,* in which Abba Kovner reads his call to resistance at the Eichmann trial in 1961.

Page 77: *Ghetto de Vilna,* 184–87.

Page 77: *Ghetto de Vilna*, 143 (first verse).
Page 79: See the introduction to the diary by Tsvi Shner, 11.

CHAPTER 3: MOSHE FLINKER

Page 82: Speech cited in J. Presser, *Ondergang. De vervolging en verdelging van het Nederlands Jodendom 1949–1945* (The Hague: Martinus Nijhoff, 1965), vol. 1, p. 267.
Page 83: Generally speaking, everything was laxer in Belgium. The country was under direct military rule, while Holland had a civilian administration over which the SS had control. In Belgium, the German military attempted, if unsuccessfully, to retain some control over the anti-Jewish activities of Himmler's death squads. Moreover, Belgian civil authorities tended to be less cooperative in complying with German directives than their Dutch counterparts, and the same was true of the leadership of Belgian Jewry. The figures speak for themselves. In contrast to Holland, with seventy-five percent of Jews killed (105,000 of 140,000 deported; about 5,000 survivors of the camps; perhaps 17,000 who survived in hiding), the survival rate of Belgian Jewry was much larger, roughly fifty percent (of 65,000 Jews in Belgium, 35,000 were interned or deported to various camps, the great majority to Auschwitz, with close to 29,000 murdered). For Belgium: "Statistique de la déportation et de l'extermination des Juifs de Belgique" in Maxime Steinberg, *L'Etoile et Le Fusil: 1942, les cent jours de la déportation des Juifs de Belgique* (Brussels: Vie Ouvrière, 1984), appendices, 239–42. As to the citations from Moshe's diary, the translation used is that of the English edition: *Young Moshe's Diary: The Spiritual Torment of a Jewish Boy in Nazi Europe*, trans. Geoffrey Wigoder (Jerusalem: Yad Vashem, 1971). This translation, for the most part, leaves out the Hebrew calendar dating, while the Dutch incorporates it. All quotations cited in Chapter 3 are based on the English edition unless otherwise noted.
Page 113: Shaul Esh's introduction to *Young Moshe's Diary*, 8.

CHAPTER 4: ÉVA HEYMAN

Page 117: A large Hungarian lake, today a popular resort area. For some of the background information, I am indebted to the introduction and notes to the English edition of the diary, *The Diary of Éva Heyman*, introduction and notes by Dr. Judah Marton, trans. Moshe M. Kohn (Jerusalem: Yad Vashem, 1963). Additional information taken from Randolph L. Braham, *The Politics of Genocide: The Holocaust in Hungary* (New York: Columbia Univeristy Press, 1981), 2 volumes; Lévai, *Black Book on the Martyrdom of Hungarian Jewry*, ed. Lawrence P. Davis (Zurich: Central European Times Publishing Company, 1948), 108; *Remember: 40 Years Since the Massacre of the Jews from Northern Transylvania under Horthyst Occupation* (Federation of Jewish Communities in the Socialist Republic of Romania, Bucharest, 1985); Maria Schmidt, "Provincial Police Reports: New Insights into Hungarian Jewish History, 1941–1944," *Yad Vashem Studies* XIX (Jerusalem, 1988); *Encyclopedia of the Holocaust* (New York: Macmillan Publishing Co., 1990), 1088–89. Alexander Leitner, "The Tragedy of the Jews in Nagyvarad (Oradea)," unpublished manuscript (Geneva, 1945), 24 (March 31, 1944); Randolph L. Braham, "The Kamenets-Podolsk and Dévidék Massacres: Prelude to the Holocaust in Hungary," *Yad Vashem Studies* IX (Jerusalem, 1978), 141.

Page 126: As it happened, Béla Zsolt did become a member of parliament in postwar Hungary, and the party he represented planned to nominate him as a minister in a coalition government. "But the coalition regime collapsed and Zsolt died in 1949." Note 48 to the diary, p. 123.

Page 127: Josephine Baker (1906–1975), African-American jazz dancer, went to Paris in the 1920s and took Europe by storm as a stage and movie star.

EPILOGUE: ANNE FRANK

Page 156: *The Diary of Anne Frank: The Critical Edition.* All quotations cited in the Epilogue are based on this source unless otherwise noted.

Page 158: Jean Schick Grossman, "Anne Frank: The Story Within Her Story," typescript (n.d.) at the Anne Frank Foundation, Amsterdam, 11.

Page 158: *"Früher wohnten wir in Frankfurt . . ."* Kleine Schriften des Historischen Museums, vol. 24 (Frankfurt-am-Main: Kleine Schriften des Historischen Museums, 1985), 60.

Page 159: *Algemeen Dagblad,* Saturday, February 4, 1984.

Page 159: "Anne Frank (1929–1945)," interview with Ben Humel, University of Groningen, 1985, 16.

Page 161: "Blue Peter" (British youth program) interview, May 10, 1976.

Page 175: Rex Brico, "Vechten tegen onbegrip" ("Combating Misunderstanding"), *Elsevier,* March 14, 1970, 96.

INDEX